BARACK OBAMA, RONALD REAGAN,

AND THE GHOST OF

DR. KING

Blogs and Essays

BARACK
OBAMA,
RONALD
REAGAN,
AND THE GHOST OF
DR. KING

Blogs and Essays

KEVIN POWELL

BARACK OBAMA, RONALD REAGAN, AND THE GHOST OF DR. KING

Blogs and Essays

Library of Congress Cataloging–in–Publication Data is available.

ISBN: 978-1-105-41409-1

Cover and interior design by Kerry DeBruce of KLAD Creative

Cover photos by Carl Posey

Printed in the United States of America

Published by Lulu Press, Inc.
3101 Hillsborough St.
Raleigh, NC 27607

www.lulu.com

10 9 8 7 6 5 4 3 2 1

Other books by Kevin Powell

In The Tradition: An Anthology of Young Black Writers
(1993; edited with Ras Baraka)

recognize
(1995; poetry)

Keepin' It Real: Post-MTV Reflections On Race, Sex, and Politics
(1997; essays)

Step Into A World: A Global Anthology of the New Black Literature
(2000; edited by Kevin Powell)

Who Shot Ya? Three Decades of Hiphop Photography
(2002; Photographs by Ernie Paniccioli/Edited by Kevin Powell)

Who's Gonna Take The Weight?
Manhood, Race, and Power in America
(2003; essays)

Someday We'll All Be Free
(2006; essays)

No Sleep Till Brooklyn: New and Selected Poems
(2008)

The Black Male Handbook: A Blueprint for Life
(2008; edited by Kevin Powell)

Open Letters to America
(2009; essays)

For the people. All people.

"I have a dream that one day every valley shall be exalted, every hill and mountain shall be made low, the rough places will be made straight and the glory of the Lord shall be revealed and all flesh shall see it together."

—*Martin Luther King, Jr.*

"There are no constraints on the human mind, no walls around the human spirit, no barriers to our progress except those we ourselves erect."

—*Ronald Reagan*

"If we aren't willing to pay a price for our values, if we aren't willing to make some sacrifices in order to realize them, then we should ask ourselves whether we truly believe in them at all."

—*Barack Obama*

CONTENTS

A Preface

This book is called *Barack Obama, Ronald Reagan, and The Ghost of Dr. King* because I believe these men are three of the most significant historical figures of the past fifty years and have, because of their unique destinies, shaped conversations in America in ways equally profound and confounding. Profound as there is no denying each, at his specific time, has been both a catalyst and a lightning rod for the raw nerves of this rocky but grand experiment we call the American democracy.

Confounding because each, as enormous in the public perception as they have been, are also incredibly imperfect leaders and men, so much so that many have worked overtime in efforts to prove they are not who we think these men are. So as I began thinking about this, my 4th essay collection and 11th book overall, it dawned on me that many of the blogs and essays were either directly or indirectly inspired by the varying impacts of Obama, Reagan, and King. In other words, I was born in the 1960s and although I have no serious memory of that decade I am very clear that I am a humble beneficiary of Dr. King and the great Civil Rights Movement. Next, my social and political awakening occurred in the 1980s at the height of the Reagan Revolution, when I was a college student and youth organizer.

That so-called revolution was an urgent challenge to many of the changes and victories of the Civil Rights era. And in this 21ˢᵗ century, this age of Obama, I am an activist, writer, public speaker, and someone who has visited 48 of America's 50 states as of this Preface because of my life work, which has given me a clear lens by which to view our nation, and its citizens.

The above means I think very hard about things I care about, be it politics, community building, sports, violence against women and girls, racism, leadership, or the national tragedy that is the murder of Trayvon Martin. That said, you should know these blogs and essays were written between 2006 and 2012. Quite a few were penned when I was running for Congress here in my adopted hometown of Brooklyn, New York. For sure, I've undergone many personal upheavals since 2006, some happiness and unquestionably some growth and progress, as well as an absurd amount of pain and tribulation. And that is precisely why I write: to make sense of the madness and chaos of my own life, of our country, of this world. That is my hope, the hope of any writer or artist, as a matter of fact, to reveal, heal, uplift, transform.

Stated differently, the goal is to get all of us—myself included—to depart from our comfort zones and to be brutally honest, difficult as it may be, about every aspect of our lives, and about the life veins that form our society. And I know that when I die I want folks to acknowledge my many faults, errors, and shortcomings. I demand that, even in life. But I also want it to be said that I was an honest human being, an honest man, and an honest writer. That I had an endless love for people, all people. And an intense passion for real freedom and real justice, that I cared and tried to do my part by being a voice for those who often feel they are voiceless.

Finally, I cannot say I have a favorite blog or essay in this collection. I will say when each was written that each felt, in that space, as the most important and urgent writing of my life. But then I always let that piece of writing go, never to be read again, and simply hope something I said, be it just a paragraph, a sentence, or a few words, is useful to you, the reader. Then I know, if that is the case, that my life work is not in vain—

KEVIN POWELL

PART **ONE**

Smells Like Teen Spirit...

Open Letter to Chris Brown

MARCH 2011
PUBLISHED IN HUFFINGTON POST

Dear Chris,

I really did not want to write this open letter, and would have preferred to speak to you in person, in private. Indeed, ever since the domestic violence incident with Rihanna two years ago, there have been attempts, by some of the women currently or formerly in your circle — women who love and care deeply about you -- to bring you and I together, as they felt my own life story, my own life experiences, might be of some help in your journey. For whatever reason, that never happened. By pure coincidence, I wound up in a Harlem recording studio with you about three months ago, as I was meeting up with R&B singer Olivia and her manager. You were hosting a listening session for your album in progress, and the room was filled with gushing supporters, with a very large security guard outside the studio door. I was allowed in, as I assume you knew my name and my long relationship to the music industry. I greeted you and said I would love to have a talk with you, but I am not even sure you heard a single word I said above the loud music. I gave your security person my card when I left and asked him to ask you to phone me, but you never did, for whatever reason. And that is fine.

But I have thought of you long and hard as I've watched you, from a distance, as you dealt with the charges of physical violence against your then-girlfriend Rihanna, as you were being pummeled by the media and abandoned by many fans, admirers and endorsers, and ridiculed on the social networks. You were 19 when the altercation with Rihanna occurred, and you are only 21 now. Yes, you've achieved both international fame and success in a way most people your age, or any age, could never imagine. But you also are at a very serious crossroads because of the dishonor of your persona derived from your beating Rihanna. There is no way to get around this, Chris. You must deal with it, as a man, now and forever. For our past can be a prison we are locked in permanently, or it can be the key to our freedom if we glean the lessons from it and deal with it directly. All the external pressures and forces will be there, Chris, but no one can free us but ourselves. And it must start in our minds and in our souls.

That is why I was very saddened to hear about your recent appearance on ABC's "Good Morning America" to promote your new album, *F.A.M.E.* The interview was embarrassing, to say the least. You slouched through the entire episode, and you were so clearly defensive as Robin Roberts, the interviewer, threw you what I thought were very easy questions about the Rihanna saga. I get that you want to move past it, but that is not going to happen, Chris, until people see real humility, real redemption and real changes in how you conduct yourself both publicly and privately. Whether the interview and what happened at ABC studios were a publicity stunt to push your album sales (as has been suggested by some blogs) is not the point. It has been spread across the internet, and throughout the world, that you ripped off your shirt following that interview, got in the face of one of the show's producers in a threatening manner, and that somehow the window in your dressing room was smashed with a chair. And then there are the photos of you immediately after, shirtless, walking outside the ABC studios looking, well, pissed off. Finally, somewhere in the midst of that morning, you tweeted, "I'm so over people bring this past s**t up!! Yet we praise Charlie Sheen and other celebs for [their] bullsh**t."

Yes, that tweet was taken down very quickly, but not before it was spread near and far, Chris. And it was a tweet written with raw honesty and, for sure, raw emotion. It is very clear to me, as it is to so many of us watching your life unfold in public, that you are deeply wounded, that you are hurt by what you have experienced the past two years. It's clear that you've never actually healed from what you witnessed as a child, either -- your mother being beaten savagely by your stepfather, and how that must've made you feel, in your bones. You've said in interviews, long before the Rihanna incident happened, that it made you scared, timid and that you wet the bed because of the wild, untamed emotions that swirled in your being. I am certain you felt powerless, just as powerless as I felt as a boy when my mother, who I love dearly and have forgiven these many years later, viciously beat me, physically and emotionally, in an effort to discipline me, to prepare me, a Black man-child, for what she, a rural South Carolina born and bred, working-class woman, perceived to be a crude and racist world.

But the fact is, Chris, we cannot afford to teach children, directly or indirectly, that violence and anger in any form are the solutions to our frustrations, disagreements or pain, and not expect that violence and anger to penetrate the psyche of that child, to not expect it to be with that child as he, you, me and countless other American males in our nation grow from boy to teenager to early adulthood. Ultimately it will come out in some channel, either inwardly on themselves in the manner of serious self-repression, self-loathing and fear, or outwardly in the shape of blind rage and violence, against themselves and against others, including women and girls.

You see, Chris, I know much about you because I was you in previous chapters of my life. I am presently in my 40s, a practitioner of yoga and someone who has spent much of the past 20 years in therapy and counseling sessions. I shudder to think who I would be today had I not made a commitment to constant self-reflection and healing. Yes, like most human beings, I do get angry at times, but it is in a very different kind of way. I think long and hard about my words and actions, and if I do make a mistake and offend someone in some way verbally or emotionally, I apologize as quickly as I can. And I am proud to say I have not been involved in a violent incident in many years, that I am about love, peace and nonviolence now, and this is my path for the rest of my life. I am not willing to go backwards, nor am I going to permit anyone or any scenario to take me backwards, either.

But, Chris, it was not always like this for me. The hurt and pain I felt as a child led to arguments and fights in my grade and high schools -- arguments with teachers and principals and physical fights with my classmates, this in spite of the fact I possessed, very early on, the same kind of talents you had coming up. Mine is writing and yours is music. And because we both had gifts that people recognized, the more problematic sides of our personas were often overlooked, or ignored completely. In reality, Chris, I attended four grade schools and three high schools partly because my single mother and I (I am an only child) were very poor, and were forced to move a lot, and partly because of my behavioral issues at various schools. Many adults could not understand it because I was routinely a straight-A student breezing through everything from math, and science, to English.

Yet I was no different from countless American children terrorized by their environments, with no true outlets to understand, and heal, what we were experiencing. That is why, Chris, I eventually was kicked out of Rutgers University, why I got into arguments with my cast mates on the first season of MTV's "The Real World," and why I often had beefs with my co-workers, as a 20-something hot shot writer at Quincy Jones' *Vibe* magazine, and why I was eventually fired from *Vibe*, Chris, in spite of writing more cover stories than any other writer in the magazine's history. There was always a darkness in my life, Chris, a heavy sadness, born of years of wounds piled one on top of the other. And I did not begin to grasp this until a fateful day in July 1991 when I pushed my girlfriend at the time into a bathroom door in the middle of an argument. As I have written in other spaces, Chris, when she ran from the apartment, barefoot, it was only then that I recognized the magnitude of what I had done. Just like you, I had to deal with public embarrassment, and court and a restraining order. But the big difference, Chris, is that a community of people, both women and men, saw potential in me, the boy struggling to be a man, in the early 1990s, and rather than shun me or push me aside or write me off completely, they instead opted to help me.

The first step was returning to therapy, as I had done briefly in 1988 after being suspended from Rutgers for threatening a female student. The next step was my struggling to take ownership for every aspect of my life, and not just that bathroom door incident. That meant, Chris, I had to go very far into my own soul, and return, time and again, to being that little boy who had been violated and abused, and meet him, on his terms. I assure you, Chris, it was extremely difficult to do that, and I put off many issues for months, even years, unwilling or unable to look myself in the mirror. Add to that the sudden celebrity of my life on MTV and at *Vibe*, and I found myself around many other people who were living escapist lives, who were not bothering to deal with their demons, either. That, Chris, is a recipe for disaster, for a life stuck in a state of arrested development. The worst thing we could ever do is to be only in circles of people who are wallowing in their own miseries, too, yet covering it up with fame, money, material things, sex, drugs, alcohol and an addiction to acting out because that is much easier than actually growing up.

As a matter of fact, as I watched your "Good Morning America" interview, and read the accounts of what happened after, I thought a good deal about the late Tupac Shakur, who I interviewed more than any other journalist when he was alive. Tupac was, Chris, without question, equally the most brilliant and the most frustrating interview subject I'd ever encountered -- brilliant because his abilities as an actor were towering (imagine what he could have been had he lived), and his writing skills instantly connected him with the man-child in so many American males, especially those of us who grew up as he did, without a consistent and available father figure or mentor, and with some form of turmoil in our lives. But, Chris, I could see the writing on the wall of Tupac's downfall from the very beginning, because he willingly participated in it, encouraged it, openly advertised it every single time he rhymed about dying, or spoke about a short shelf life in one of his interviews. I do believe each and every one of us human beings is given a certain amount of time on this planet. I for one feel very blessed to be here as long as I have been, especially given my past destructive paths. But I also believe, Chris, that so many of us participate in what I call self-sabotage, or slow suicide. That is, because we do not have the emotional and spiritual tools to process the many angles of our lives, we instead resort to predictable behavior that may feel empowering or liberating on the surface, but is actually damaging to us, and doing even more harm to us.

For instance, when I looked at the photo of you, shirtless, with the shiny tattoos across your chest, I saw myself, I saw Tupac Shakur, I saw all us American Black boys who so badly want to be free, who so badly want to be understood, who feel life is unfair for labeling us "angry," "difficult," "violent," "abusive," "criminals," "cocky" or "arrogant." Yes, Chris Brown, in spite of Barack Obama being President of the United States, America still very much has a very serious problem with race and racism, which means it still has a very serious problem with Black males who act out or behave badly, who speak their minds, who assert themselves in some way or another. I know that is what you are reacting to, Chris. And you are not wrong in tweeting that Charlie Sheen is catching a break in a way that you are not. I am aware that Charlie Sheen's father is Latino and his mother is White, but Charlie Sheen operates in a space of White male privilege because of his White skin and his access to White power. Thus he is given a pass for his violent, abusive, mean-spirited, and drug-addicted outbursts in a way you or I never will, Chris. Charlie Sheen, as insane as it appears, is even celebrated in many circles because of how American male (read: White male) privilege can exist while ignoring the concerns of those he has harmed, including women.

That is why, Chris, I rarely discuss in public the chapter of my life that is MTV's "The Real World." In spite of who I am as a whole human being, my numerous interests and skill sets, the one thing that was played up were the arguments I had with my White cast mates. So I was labeled, for years and years, Chris, as "the angry Black man," something that troubled me as deeply as you were bothered on "Good Morning America" by the Rihanna questions. And how certain media folks, including Joy Behar on "The View," must bother you calling you a "thug," in spite of the obvious racial overtones of such a loaded word. If you are a thug, then what is Charlie Sheen, or Mel Gibson, or John Mayer, or Jude Law, or any other famous White male who has engaged in bad behavior the past few years? Why are they often forgiven, given a pass, allowed to clean themselves up and to redeem themselves in a way Black males simply cannot, Chris? It is because, to paraphrase Tupac, we were given this world, we did not make it. And it is because of power, Chris, plain and simple. Whoever has the power to put forth images and words, to put forth definitions, to determine what is right and what is wrong, can just as easily label you a star one day and a thug and a has-been the very next day; or make you, a Black male, the poster child, for every single bad behavior that exists in America. Just ask Black males as diverse as Tiger Woods, Kobe Bryant, Mike Tyson, O.J. Simpson or Kanye West. No apologies are being made by me for these men or their actions, but the chatter, always, in Black male circles is how we are treated when we do wrong as opposed to how our White brothers are treated when they do wrong. Call it racial or cultural paranoia if you'd like. We Black brothers call it a ridiculously oppressive double standard. And that is because America has historically had a very complicated and twisted relationship with Black men, ranging from slavery, to the first heavyweight boxing champion Jack Johnson, to Malcolm X and Dr. King both, and including men like Louis Armstrong, Chuck Berry, Michael Jackson, Prince and, yes, Barack Obama. Sometimes we feel incredible love and affection, and sometimes we feel as if we are unwanted, armed and dangerous. It is a schizophrenic existence, to say the least, and it is akin to how the character Bigger Thomas, in Richard Wright's classic but controversial novel, *Native Son,* saw his life reduced to the metaphor of a cornered black rat. Thus so many of us spend our entire lives, as Black males, navigating this tricky terrain, so few of us with the proper emotional and spiritual tools to balance our coolness with a righteous defiance that, well, will not get us killed, literally and figuratively, by each other or the police, or by the American mass media culture.

I am telling you the truth, Chris Brown, man-to-man, Black man to Black man, because you need to hear it -- straight up, no chaser. If you really believe that because you are famous and successful that the same rules apply to you, you are deceiving yourself. Like many, I love people, regardless of race, gender, class, sexual orientation, disability, religion, any of that, and I believe deeply in the humanity and equality of us all. But until we have a nation, and a world, where the media places the same energy and excitement in documenting a Black man who is engaging in, say, mentoring work, as it does in a Black man smashing a window at a television station, then we are sadly fooling ourselves, Chris, that things are fair and equal in this universe. They are not. And sometimes it will be big things, like what you just experienced, Chris, at "Good Morning America," and sometimes it will be quieter moments, far off the radar, where we Black men have to think on the fly about who we are, what we represent, how others perceive us or may want to perceive us, how we say things to people, particularly our White sisters and brothers, for fear or worry of being misunderstood and being pegged as "problematic" or a "troublemaker," and magically navigate best we can to assert our humanity, our dignity, our leadership, our visions and ideas and dreams, and, yes, our definitions of manhood rooted in our very unique cultural journeys. Complete insanity, this emotional and spiritual juggling act, no question, and our harsh reality in this world, my friend.

So what you have to understand, Chris, and what I had to grapple with for years, is there is no escaping your past, especially if we engage in angry or violent behavior. If we do not confront it, probe and understand it, heal and learn from it, and use what we've learned to teach others to go a different way, then it dogs us forever, Chris, and we unwittingly become the entertainment, nonstop, for others. And that simply does not have to be the case for you, Chris. You are too much of a genius to allow this to destroy you, but your self-destruction is exactly what many of us are witnessing. I have no idea who is around you at this point, or what kind of men, specifically, are advising you, but the worst possible thing you could do is act as if what happened with Rihanna was no big deal. It was and is a major deal because women and girls, in America, and on this earth, are beaten, stabbed, shot, murdered, raped and molested, every single day. Because of your fame you have become, unfortunately, a poster child for this destructive behavior in spite of your proclaiming just a few years before, in a magazine interview, you would never do to a woman what had happened to your mother. What I gathered, very quickly, Chris, after I pushed that girlfriend back in 1991, was that I could not hide from my demons or myself. That is why I wrote an essay in

Essence magazine in September 1992, entitled, "The Sexist in Me." That is why I made it a point to listen to women and girls in my travels, in my community, even within my family, tell stories of how they had been violated or abused by one man or another. And that is why, Chris, nearly 20 years later, so much of my work as a leader, as an activist, as a public speaker, is dedicated to ending violence against women and girls. In other words, I took what was a very negative and hurtful experience, for that girlfriend, and for myself, and transformed it into a life of teaching other males how to deal with their hurts without hurting others, particularly women and girls.

Tupac Shakur, Chris, never got to turn the corner, as you well know, because he was gunned down at age 25. I do not know if he actually raped or sexually assaulted the woman in that hotel room as he was charged. But one thing he did admit to me, Chris, in that famous Rikers Island interview, was that he could have stopped his male friends from coming into his hotel room and sexually exploiting his female companion that night. And he did not. You, Chris Brown, cannot turn back the hands of time to February 2009. We have seen the photos of Rihanna's battered and bruised face. Yes, you've apologized; yes, you've done your time in court and your hours of community service; and yes, you have been tried and convicted in the court of public opinion. But it is really up to you, Chris, to decide in these tense moments, as you approach your 22nd birthday May 5th, if you want to be a boy forever locked in the time capsule of your own battered and bruised life, or if you want to be the man so many of us are rooting for you to be, one who will take responsibility for all his actions, who will sit up in interviews and answer all questions, even the uncomfortable ones, the kind of man who will admit, once and for all, publicly, privately, however you must do it, that you need help, that you need love, that you need to love yourself in a very different kind of way, that you no longer will hide behind an album release, music videos, dyed hair, tattoos or even your Twitter account, Chris Brown. That you will make a life-long commitment to counseling, to therapy, to healing, to alternative definitions of manhood rooted in nonviolence, love and peace, that you will become a loud and consistent voice against all forms of violence against women and girls, wherever you go, as I do, for the rest of your life. All eyes are on you because you've brought the world to your doorstep, my friend. The question, alas, Chris, is do you want to go forward, or not? And if "yes" to going forward, then you must know it means going to the deepest and darkest parts of your past to heal what ails you, once and for all, for the good of yourself, and for the good of those who are watching you very closely and who may learn something from what you do. Or what you do not do. The choice is yours, Chris Brown. The choice is yours.

Godspeed,
Kevin Powell

Arizona is America

JANUARY 2011
PUBLISHED IN HUFFINGTON POST

I   say this because Arizona is not the problem. We the people are the problem.

That is, we Americans who think it is cool to engage in rhetoric, political or otherwise, that encourages division, ugliness, hatred, and violence, directly or indirectly.

Over the past several years, we've witnessed this madness via certain television networks, TV and radio talk shows, the internet, and various rallies and protests: a climate of hatred and, yes, violence, which has been boiling, with a quickness, in our America.

This is not about left versus right political philosophies, nor Democrats versus Republicans, or progressives versus Tea Party followers, or about the wackness of Arizona, a state that once, aided by one of its senators, John McCain, refused to celebrate the Dr. King holiday after it was made a federal law (to be fair, Mr. McCain eventually backed away from that position).

Not per se.

KEVIN POWELL

But it is about any of us who are so politically, emotionally, and spiritually immature that the only way we know how to participate in dialogue on any issue is to scream, curse, or otherwise threaten and dehumanize each other. Or move to murder each other. Quite literally.

Add to this cruel reality show the new world order our technological revolution has birthed in the form of the social networks, and you suddenly have these spaces where an angry and misguided individual or groups of angry and misguided people can post the most anti-social pronouncements imaginable, grow an audience, and prepare, right in front of our very eyes, to unleash their rage on unsuspecting and innocent persons.

So, yes, it pains me that Congresswoman Gabrielle Giffords was shot in the head at point-blank range by 22-year-old Jared Lee Loughner in Arizona. Painful, too, that 19 others were wounded and 6 are dead, including John M. Roll, the chief judge for the United States District Court for Arizona, and a 9-year-old girl named Christina Green.

According to Christina's mother Roxanna Green, mother and daughter were there at that Tucson, Arizona area Safeway parking lot because her daughter was interested in government and wanted to learn how to give back to the community. A little girl full of life's possibilities blown away by a young man mentally unstable enough to believe he could change the course of history, with a gun I am sure he was able to purchase rather easily.

As a result there will be no giving back for little Christina ever again because no one can give that child another breath.

But what we can do is heed the words of Clarence Dupnik, the Pima County sheriff at a press conference:

"The anger, the hatred, the, uh, bigotry that goes on in this country, is getting to be outrageous. And, unfortunately, Arizona has sort of become the capital. We have become the mecca for prejudice and bigotry."

Well, yes, indeed, when you review, say, the horrible anti-immigration sentiments there. Plus the fact that the late Judge Roll had to accept protection from the Federal Marshals Service in 2009. This was in response to his allowing to proceed a civil rights lawsuit by a group of Mexicans against an Arizona rancher who thought it his right to stop people at gunpoint as they crossed his land, then turn them over to the Border Patrol.

Regardless of where you may fall on the issue of immigration, pointing guns at other human beings, or outright shooting them (which has occurred often in those parts), is simply not the way. Nor is threatening the life of a federal judge because you do not agree with his decision. Says that we are not quite the fair and egalitarian civilization we claim to be, at best. Says some of us are barbaric, at worst.

Beyond Arizona, nor is it acceptable for the flames of anger and venom to be blown, mightily, at those Summer 2009 townhall meetings on the pending healthcare legislation.

Nor has it been acceptable the barely masked threats against President Barack Obama, a constant stream of verbal aggression so nasty that you wonder if someone wants to do total harm to his presidency, just because—

Nor is it acceptable for Sarah Palin's website to not merely list 20 vulnerable Democrats to target in 2010, but to have the picture of a gun crosshair displayed for each of the 20, including Congresswoman Giffords.

Nor is it acceptable for The Tea Party to condemn the Tucson shooting (while scrambling fast to state Jared Lee Loughner is not one of them) but still not have the moral courage, nor outrage, to condemn, once and for all, its own oratory, these many months of its movement, that dance right at the doorstep of political anarchy and, yes, violence.

For when we use the words and images of violence, be we on the left or those of us on the right, we invite violence right into our lives, even if it is a moderate Congressional member simply hosting an outdoor gathering to meet her voters on a weekend trip back to her district. Because once you've fostered, egged on, and actually kick-started a violent atmosphere and a violent mindset, there is no sacred ground in our America, and you will not be free from violence and tragedies, be it in the ghettos or in the suburbs.

And as long as there is an incredible addiction to violence in America—ranging from averting our eyes from the regular practice of domestic violence against women to our acquiescence in unnecessary wars overseas, to our love affair with violent blockbuster films and video games, to this twisted need to define our culture (especially we men and boys) through the barrel of a gun, you come to the clear-eyed conclusion that violence, as one 1960s activist put it matter of factly, is as American as apple pie.

But it does not have to be. But only if we Americans are

collectively willing to be morally responsible enough, and mature enough, to engage in conversations that do not seek to hurt or destroy others, just because you may not like them or their views. In our American journey we've witnessed violence against Native Americans, Blacks, poor and ethnic Whites, women and girls, the handicapped and the disabled, gay, lesbian, and transgender individuals, Latino and Asian immigrants, Arabs and Muslims, Jews (it is not lost on me that Representative Giffords is the first female Congressional member from the state of Arizona), and more members of the human family than we could list in this blog.

It is seemingly the preferred way, to resort to violence when we believe everything else has failed, when we feel alienated, angry, and confused, as evidenced by Jared Lee Loughner's internet postings (as was the case with the Columbine shooters in Colorado back in the day). Or when we feel our way of life, our way of viewing the world, is threatened.

For example, when I hear some Americans say they want their country back, that they want things the way they once were, I as an African American often wonder, Want your country back for whom? And, The way things once were for whom? If we followed that logic I would be, say, my long-dead grandfather: not able to look White males or females in the eyes for fear of violent punishment; having to jump off the curb if a White person were walking in my direction; and my life reduced to work in someone else's cotton or tobacco field, or as a source of cheap, service-oriented labor, and my life permanently imprisoned by poverty and no hope whatsoever. If that or any other brand of social injustice is not a form of violence, then I do not know what it is.

So part of this unraveling of violence in our society, too, has to do with all of us, of every race and culture and gender and faith and class and sexual orientation, having the chutzpah to talk shop about our country, mountaintops of mistakes included, both past and present. In other words, in order for us to have a future not completely defined by violence, anger, and finger-pointing, I am essentially calling for a very necessary kind of soul-searching that America needs to do before what happened to Congresswoman Giffords becomes as routine as the too-many-to-count assassinations and assassination attempts we witnessed in the 1960s and 1970s.

In our America—

The Super Bowl and Violence Against Females

FEBRUARY 2011
PUBLISHED IN THE WOMEN'S MEDIA CENTER

I have been a sports fan for as long as I can remember. As a youth I formally played baseball, ran track and boxed until I decided I really valued my brain cells more than winning a bout; and informally we boys on the block played stickball, soccer, football (sometimes even tackling each other on concrete), basketball, and anything else that required us to run, hit, catch, or fall.

In fact, I am a writer partially because of sports. When I was a boy of no more than 8 or 9, my mother began the practice of taking me to the Jersey City Public Library, the Greenville Branch, as often as she could, usually on Saturdays as that was her day off from work. My mother would sift and read through the local newspaper while my imagination and I were allowed to run wild amongst the stacks of books. And the first ones that grabbed my attention were sports books. About the history of my beloved New York Yankees. About the golden eras

KEVIN POWELL

of baseball and football. I memorized a plethora of facts and figures because these larger-than-life characters, with names like Red Granger and Joe DiMaggio, and Jackie Robinson and Jim Brown, were utterly heroic and magical to me. Without a doubt I was so enthralled with sports that I made it a point to watch every televised baseball or football game I could, and actually learned the rules to almost every single sport, including ones I did not play, like tennis, golf, or hockey, just because.

And outside of the World Series, the Super Bowl was the spectacle to anticipate every single year. The very first one I watched, as a child, was Super Bowl X between the Dallas Cowboys and the Pittsburgh Steelers. That game is the reason why I became a Cowboys fan for over two decades (today I root strictly for New York area sports teams), although the Steelers won because of those acrobatic catches of game MVP Lynn Swann.

I have not missed a Super Bowl since, 34 years and counting. I saw Jackie Smith drop a potential game-winning touchdown for the Cowboys in the rematch with the Steelers a couple of seasons later. I saw Jim Plunkett raise from the dead his career and create a legacy for himself as a Raider. I saw Joe Montana coolly win four Super Bowl rings of his own. I saw Doug Williams become the first and only Black quarterback to lead his team (the Washington Redskins) to a Super Bowl victory. I saw the Buffalo Bills lose four consecutive Super Bowls, undermining their great Marv Levy-coached teams. And I saw my New York Giants shock the New England Patriots, and the world, via David Tyree's supernatural "helmet catch," crushing the Pats quest for an undefeated season. Truth be told, the Super Bowl has become as integral a part of American culture as Christmas, "I Love Lucy" reruns, Coca-Cola, Disney movies, and the music of the Gershwins. It is an unofficial holiday for us, and, in many ways, our post-modern edition of the Last Supper.

Yet something has, admittedly, been radically different for me since those heady days of being a reckless, violent man-child. Twenty years ago this year I pushed a then-girlfriend into a bathroom door in our shared apartment. And my life was altered forever, as I have written in other spaces (see my essay "Ending Violence Against Women and Girls": *http:// www.huffingtonpost.com/kevin-powell/ending-violence-against-w_b_70585.html*. Twenty years removed from that sort of behavior, thanks to therapy, healing, the forgiveness of many, including the woman I violated, and an activist's life which these days includes consistent writings, speeches, and work to end violence against women and girls, I soak up sports, especially football, not just as a fan, but as someone deeply concerned with the human condition. For sports is, and has always been, a metaphor for our lives.

And because I, you, we, would be lying to ourselves if we did not confess that football, as electrifying and audacious as it is, is also a brutally violent sport. So violent, in fact, that many former players are permanently damaged physically, and a fair share emotionally, too, due to concussions or other head traumas. (No coincidence, then, that just this past season the NFL passed out numerous fines for what it deemed excessively vicious hits.) But what has particularly given me pause, as a man with an acute awareness of sexism and gender violence, is the steady convoy of NFL players being accused or arrested, year to year, season to season, for an act of aggression against a woman. These charges and allegations have ranged from domestic violence and rape to actual murder. And these are merely the incidents that have become public.

More to the point, there is the glaring state of affairs, right in our faces during these Super Bowl sweepstakes, of the game's two-time champion quarterback, Ben Roethlisberger. I certainly give Big Ben, as he is known, his props as a clutch quarterback, and fully acknowledge that if the Steelers win on Sunday it will be because of Roethlisberger's play and his unquestioned knack for staying in the pocket, even at risk to his own health. But Big Ben also happens to be the most high-profile player, in recent memory, accused of sexual assault on two different occasions, one claim occurring less than a year ago. The accuser, a then-20-year-old student at a Georgia college, was seen at several establishments with Roethlisberger leading up to the incident, including posing for a photograph with him. Roethlisberger spoke with police the night of the incident and stated that he did have contact with the woman that was not "consummated," and afterward the accuser slipped and injured her head.

The woman alleged that Roethlisberger, after inviting her and her friends to the V.I.P. area of the nightclub, encouraged them to do numerous shots of alcohol before one of his bodyguards—an off-duty officer, led her down a hallway to a stool and left. Roethlisberger allegedly approached and exposed himself and, despite the woman's protests, followed her into what turned out to be a bathroom when she tried to leave through the first door she saw. The woman claims Roethlisberger then had sex with her. It is further alleged that friends of the woman attempted to intervene out of worry, but the second of Roethlisberger's bodyguards, an off-duty Pennsylvania State Trooper, avoided eye contact and said he did not know what they were talking about. The policemen later claimed to "have no memory" of meeting the woman.

The incident brought a great deal of embarrassment to the NFL and to the proud Pittsburgh Steelers franchise. Although Roethlisberger was never charged with a crime, the NFL still suspended him for the first six games of the 2010 season (it was later reduced to four games). Steelers president Art Rooney II was said to be "furious" about Roethlisberger's situation, and Big Ben lost a number of endorsements and supporters. The accuser did not go forth with the case because she did not want to be subjected to the huge media and public spotlight, but she has also stood by her account of what happened.

At his Super Bowl media conference this week, Big Ben never directly addressed this or another instance where he was alleged to have committed sexual assault against a woman. What he did say is "You make mistakes in life and you learn from them. And I think that's what I'm doing now."

While I, given my own history, would be the first to say we should offer every single human being who makes a mistake a shot at redemption, the hope, perhaps naively on my part, is that Big Ben, and the NFL in general, would, once and for all, condemn violence against women, mainly because one too many pro football players have been getting into trouble with the law because of how they mistreat women. I am not trying to single out Commissioner Roger Goodell and the National Football League, but the hard fact is, according to CNN, more than 100 million people will watch the Super Bowl on any given Sunday in early February. That presents a really unique and grand opportunity for our athletes, huge influencers on the behavior of younger and older folks who idolize and worship them, to take a position. The NFL and other major sports leagues already do it on the issue of breast cancer, and this matter is just as significant. Indeed, it is one of the most important civil and human rights issues of the 21st century.

Especially given the multiple reports and news clips saying that "pimps" will traffic thousands of under-age prostitutes to Texas for Sunday's Super Bowl, hoping to do business with men arriving for the big game with money to burn. Although it is difficult to pinpoint an exact number, it is believed that thousands of underage girls have been brought to recent Super Bowls to engage male customers in sex. What we do know for sure is that up to 300,000 girls between 11 and 17 years of age are lured into the American sex industry annually, according to a 2007 report sponsored by the Department of Justice and written by the nonprofit group Shared Hope International. At the end of the day this human trafficking of these young girls is simply another version of violence against females.

The other equally critical issue is how we American males define manhood. Far too many of us think it is about violent behavior, warfare, gunplay, mindless and ego-driven competition, and the conquering of each other, or women and girls, by any available means. And this has nothing to do with the debates that have raged for years about there being a spike in domestic violence cases on Super Bowl Sundays because of the drinking and abusive behavior of male sports fans. Hard to pin down that kind of data. But it unquestionably is a day when so many different types of people come together, pause, and watch perhaps America's bloodiest and most violent sport as if it were a video game. How incredible would it be to use the saga of Ben Roethlisberger as a teachable moment? For boys and young men: violence in any form against women and girls is completely unacceptable, including forcing yourself sexually upon a female. For girls and young women: under no circumstances whatsoever should a man or boy strike, hit, beat, or otherwise seek to bring you bodily harm. For males and females alike: How can we condemn the treatment of women and girls in foreign countries yet say little to nothing as female minors are being trafficked during Super Bowl Week for the pleasure of sexually despicable American males who could easily be these girls' fathers or grandfathers?

Beyond what we say or do as citizens who care, star athletes and professional leagues like the NFL have got to muster the courage of a Joe Torre, the former long-time New York Yankees manager and guaranteed Hall of Famer: he has spoken eloquently, as an adult, about the domestic violence his mother suffered at the hands of his father when he was growing up. This has become a mission for Mr. Torre, and we really need a generation of athletes to combat this scourge that happens in American communities daily. That is why it is so great that Dallas Cowboy Pro Bowler Jay Ratliff, in the past few days, made a public service announcement entitled "Real men don't buy children. They don't buy sex."

And real men don't hit beat berate sexually assault rape or seek to humiliate women either. Conceivably this is why, with regards to Big Ben, I have gotten a number of tweets and emails from women saying there is no way they will root for the Pittsburgh Steelers on Sunday, because they feel Roethlisberger was given a slap on the wrist and is once again enjoying the fruits of being a man with privilege in our still very sexist society. They are right, of course, and this will not change unless a superstar athlete with the shine and stage of a Big Ben takes a very public stand in the movement to end violence and sexual assault against women and girls with the same sort of guts that, say, Muhammad Ali displayed in his stand against the Vietnam War. In other words, we need to be able to cheer for our star athletes outside the arena as much as we do inside. And cheer for them in a way that is about so much more than the sport they play or the championships they win—

Kool Herc, Hiphop, and Healthcare

FEBRUARY 2011
PUBLISHED IN DAILY KOS

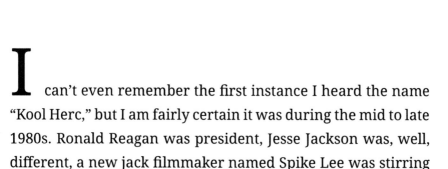

I can't even remember the first instance I heard the name "Kool Herc," but I am fairly certain it was during the mid to late 1980s. Ronald Reagan was president, Jesse Jackson was, well, different, a new jack filmmaker named Spike Lee was stirring the pot called Hollywood, and I was a young and avid "hiphop head."

Ever since I digested the boom-bap strands of hiphop in the late 1970s in my native Jersey City, New Jersey (my hometown's local hiphop heroes was a crew called Sweet, Slick, and Sly) I was hooked. The Sugar Hill Gang's landmark song "Rapper's Delight," which I would later learn plagiarized lyrics from Grandmaster Caz of the legendary Cold Crush Brothers, was the shot heard 'round the world. Kurtis Blow was hiphop's first solo superstar. Afrika Bambaataa was the spiritual and musical emissary from funk and soul to hiphop. Grandmaster Flash and The Furious Five spoke so poignantly to my then-ghetto existence that I cried, hard, the first time I heard "The Message." And Run-DMC was for us bboys and bgirls what The Beatles had been for screaming White teens two decades earlier.

Fitted Lee Jeans with stitched creases, suede Pumas, Le Tigre shirts, Kangols, name belts, baseball caps with sketched designs in the front folded on top with paper stuffed inside thus the caps floated on our heads like royal crowns, magic markers in our front or back pockets so we could tag our names here there everywhere (my tag was my nickname, "kepo1"), and so many of us popping locking breaking moonwalking doing the Pee Wee Herman the trot the wop the smurf the running man. We had no idea we were in the middle of a cultural revolution, but that is exactly what it was. And I am sure most of us did not know it was Kool Herc who kick-started the whole thing.

Right after my high school years I left Jersey City and went to college at Rutgers University where I would stumble upon the anti-apartheid movement, Black and Latino history in ways I had never contemplated previously, an upper class student named Lisa Williamson who would later change her name to Sister Souljah, and a spirit of activism that has been with me ever since. Indeed, we did not call it "hiphop activism" back then, but that is precisely what folks like myself, Souljah, Ras Baraka, April Silver, and many other Black and Latino babies of the Civil Rights Movement were doing, to a hiphop beat. Organizing in welfare hotels in mid-town Manhattan; building a summer camp for poor youth in North Carolina; re-registering voters in the Deep South; marching against police brutality here there everywhere; and staging state of the youth rallies and concerts in Harlem and Brooklyn.

It was somewhere between my trips to clubs with names like The Rooftop, Union Square, and Funhouse, and that work as a youth and student organizer, that his name first pushed its way into my consciousness:

Kool Herc, the father of hiphop—

But the details were sketchy at best:

- Born in Jamaica as Clive Campbell.
- Came to America in the late 1960s, on the heels of the Civil Rights Movement.
- Heavily influenced by great artists of the funk and soul era, including James Brown.
- Lived in The Bronx, one of New York City's five boroughs, and the birthplace of hiphop culture.
- Earned his nickname, "Hercules," because of his height, frame, and demeanor on the basketball court as a youth. It was later shortened to Herc. And DJ Kool Herc & The Herculoids would become one of the early groundbreaking hiphop acts.
- Along with Afrika Bambaataa and Grandmaster Flash widely considered the founding fathers, and the holy trinity of hiphop.
- Generally credited with creating "the break beat" in the early 1970s, a djing technique that forms a critical foundation for hiphop music.

And that is essentially what I would know until far into the 1990s, when I first met Kool Herc in person at one or another hiphop program attempting to make hiphop into the political movement it never was, and that it will never be.

For hiphop is a cultural movement with political roots and

political overtones, no question, but I have always been clear, even as a youth, that leaders have to emerge from hiphop's multiple generations who, while nurtured on hiphop culture, must engage and work with the artists and iconic figures of our day just the way, say, Malcolm X engaged Sam Cooke, Maya Angelou, and Muhammad Ali or Martin Luther King, Jr. engaged Aretha Franklin and Harry Belafonte. Artists, cultural icons, can highlight, reflect, and support a movement, but those of us with real organizing skills and consistent activist mindsets must be the ones to make movements happen. The artists inspire activists to do what we do, and we activists inspire the artists to do what they do. And every now and then a great artist also happens to also be a great activist. (Think of Bono of the rock group U2, or Chuck D, front man for Public Enemy.)

That, for sure, is what we were doing in the late 1980s and early 1990s here in New York City, and in other parts of America. Making a movement go as we connected with everyone from LL Cool J and MC Lyte to Doug E Fresh and Ice Cube. But somewhere things went awry, many of us young activists fell off and out of the work for the people, and what we thought was a burgeoning social movement for change, fueled by hiphop, got decimated by a shift in what the corporations were suddenly permitting to be marketed and sold, with enthusiasm. Or not. In other words, ever since the early 1990s we've had those of us who represent hiphop culture, with its five core elements (djing, mcing, dancing, graffiti writing, and knowledge). And then there is the hiphop industry, the bastard child of the culture, manipulated, twisted, and bent out of shape by a few corporations more interested in a dollar bill than the holistic development and natural growth of this art form. That is why we've been bombarded with over-the-top cursing and use of the N word, glorified violence, sexism and a ruthless disrespect for women and girls, excessive materialism, and soft porn and gangsterism passing as music videos for far too long. I am a writer, an artist myself, so I do not believe in censorship in any form. I am also a history buff, so I know full well our society is riddled with racism, sexism, violence, anti-intellectualism, and materialism, and that hiphop did not create any of these things. Hiphop, being the dominant cultural expression it is, simply is the most immediate and accessible frame flashing, 100 beats per minute, what is very wrong in too many to count American 'hoods, both urban and suburban.

Likewise, what I do believe is missing is balance. Yes, I am absolutely clear that hiphop is a multicultural movement, belonging to people of all races, ethnicities, cultures, throughout the globe. And I love that I have come across, say, Israeli and Palestinian hiphoppers using the music to talk peace, or Italian, German, or French hiphoppers learning English via the music, or South African or Latin American hiphoppers using it as a tool for social change, or Asian American hiphoppers in California who love, embrace, and represent the culture far more than the offspring of the founders do. But the harsh reality is that the images we see, the sagas of mayhem we hear most, are of Black and Latino people. This is not just damaging to our psyches, just as crack cocaine was, but it is damaging to our spirits. And we've become stuck in a very vicious cycle where I sometimes wonder how many of us truly grasp that there is nothing wrong with rhyming about the ghetto, about parties and material things, if we also are expanding our worldviews enough to discuss other concerns, too. But that can't happen if specific gatekeepers in the industry game block that kind of personal and cultural evolution from occurring. A Lil' Wayne, talented and fascinating as he is, is put on a mighty big pedestal because he is not really saying much at all and has become a cartoonish figure merely there for entertainment and shock value. Meanwhile, someone as intelligent and insightful as a Talib Kweli has to grind, hard, just for airplay, gigs, and our Twitter attention spans. As long as that kind of awful imbalance exists, then you can bet your bottom buck that Kool Herc and every other hiphop pioneer are not a part of conversations around the state of hiphop, the culture or the industry.

And just as there is a huge gap between older folks who know and can speak to the social struggles of bygone eras and the youth who often do not know those tales, there too is a huge gap between we heads who understand the history and traditions of hiphop, and those who actually believe it must've begun with Tupac or The Notorious B.I.G. I wish I were exaggerating, but the things I have heard in my travels across America about what hiphop is or is not are often, at best, numbing. No fault of our own, it is simply not taught in the schools, as it should be at this point. And God knows very few grade or high schools, or colleges or universities, ever consider bringing a living, breathing hiphop legend in to guest lecture, to be an artist in residence, especially given how much hiphop music and culture have penetrated every single crevice of American society.

And that is why quite a few who claim to love and be hiphop do not even know who Kool Herc is. And why those who have benefited, culturally, spiritually, and, yes, monetarily, have rarely engaged him from this thing we call hiphop. And this thing called hiphop, which was, for the most part, created by poor, working-class African Americans, West Indians, and Latinos in New York City, with a parallel energy generated by Latinos and Black on the West Coast in the 1970s, is now a multi-billion dollar global industry, and the dominant cultural expression on the planet for 30plus years and counting.

That, I imagine, is why Kool Herc and other pioneers of hiphop have always made it a point to stand up at various hiphop-related events and state who they are—sometimes with love and respect, sometimes with shades of bitterness and resentment framing the edges of their mouths—because if they do not, then they would remain largely invisible, or completely ignored. Think about how, for example, Black basketball trailblazers from back in the day, the ones documented in that great ESPN film "Black Magic," must feel when they hear of the millions a LeBron James can command because of the sweat and blood equity they put in when there was no cable television, no endorsement deals, and these players were just as likely to be the victims of racial injustices as cheers.

As a matter of fact, I recall when I curated the very first exhibit on the history of hiphop culture in America, at the Rock and Roll Hall of Fame, in 1999, I encountered this kind of weariness, born of years of neglect, on numerous occasions. But I also remember the great joy many of these hiphop legends displayed because they were being recognized for their contributions. Unfortunately, that exhibit was so woefully under-funded, that we had to scrape together sponsors as best we could just to mount the show and fly pioneers there. For all the billions of dollars hiphop has made our economy and certain corporate giants, the great irony is how some still don't view it as a legitimate art form, then and now. Regardless, as you can imagine, it was profoundly moving to meet, one by one, the architects of hiphop. Folks with names like Lady Pink, Popmaster Fabel, Lee Quinones, and an army of others. But the one person who always had the greatest mystique around him, without question, was Kool Herc.

For the record, we need to understand that Kool Herc is to hiphop what individuals like Big Mama Thornton, Louis Jordan, Chuck Berry, and Little Richard are to the history of rock and roll. Or what Jelly Roll Morton and The Creole Band are to jazz: visionary figures that were far ahead of their time that they have been taken for granted, save a handful of diehard fans and historians.

And therein lies the enormous dilemma of Kool Herc's current health condition. According to his sister Cindy Campbell who, as long as I can remember, has always been there supporting the legacy of her brother, Herc was hospitalized last October. He has serious kidney stones and they must be removed. $10,000 worth of medical bills have been piled up, and there is a need, according to Cindy, to raise at least $25,000 to cover expenses tied to this very necessary surgical procedure.

And Kool Herc, founding father of hiphop, is like so many

dwelling in America: He does not have health insurance. Kool Herc makes his living djing and speaking, but he undoubtedly has not been treated in the way rock and jazz heroes and sheroes are treated.

Moreover, such a twisted paradox, this theme of Kool Herc's lack of healthcare coverage, as we watch lawsuit after lawsuit being filed, throughout our nation, to dismantle President Obama's historic legislation. And the Republican-dominated House of Representatives has already voted to repeal the president's healthcare reform. Although that will not happen in the Democratic-controlled Senate chamber, the House vote is, assuredly, part of a long-term strategy aimed at undermining and derailing our president's legislation.

To put this in a different context, as Kool Herc was setting foot in America in the late 1960s, Dr. King was publicly condemning the war in Vietnam and ultimately calling for "a poor people's campaign." For Dr. King understood that true democracy could never be fully realized in America if each and every one of us did not have access to the most basic of needs, including a quality education, a decent place to live, an opportunity to work, and the ability to get help if we were to take ill.

Dr. King was assassinated, and as quickly as major civil rights victories were won, conservative forces moved to dismantle or destroy them. That is why I always say to those critical of hiphop to keep in mind that if Kool Herc and others had not created this art form in the first place, there would be even more Blacks and Latinos, especially, who are unemployed, on the streets committing crimes, in jail, and without healthcare, or without anyone to petition for us to get help as hiphop icon DJ Premiere initially did for Kool Herc.

"Herc wants to use this to bring awareness, not just about healthcare," says Cindy Campbell. She adds: "There are so many other hiphop legends in similar situations, but they are not Kool Herc, so no one is going to rally around them. We want to create a foundation, a union, a fund, that makes sure these pioneers are protected in their time of need."

And that is what we who truly care need to do. I have been bombarded with facebook messages and tweets from individuals not only angry and disturbed that Kool Herc is in this position, but also that certain hiphop luminaries are not moving, quickly or at all, to cover Herc's medical bills. Names are being called. And hiphop moguls and superstars are being denigrated publicly. I personally don't think that is the way to go. If the wealthy in hiphop America want to step up, they will. I hope they do, but I am not expecting much at this point given how much our culture has deteriorated into a space of spiritual imbalance and extreme individualism at the expense of the larger hiphop world. When any people, community, or culture has been dumbed down that much by forces beyond our comprehension, then it is not difficult to get why someone as valuable as a Kool Herc is as easily discarded as one's last text message, or one's last order of fast food.

Thus, what would be much more effective is, again, that permanent fund or foundation to support hiphop pioneers and classic hiphop artists just like we see with other genres of popular music. That way we never again have one of our legends sitting without healthcare as they make their way through their 50s, 60s, and beyond.

Additionally, I echo Cindy's contention that hiphop, after all these years, needs to be recognized by our country, on a federal level, for the great cultural contributions it has made to America, and to the planet. No Kool Herc, no hiphop, and there would be no Queen Latifah, no Will Smith, no Jay-Z, no Russell Simmons, no Eminem, no mass popularity of professional basketball, no swagger to President Obama's walk, no street teams as a marketing concept, and no spice to our American vocab (Do we really think catchphrases like "I'm good" just fall from the sky?).

Similarly, my friend, Toni Blackman, is not only one of the best freestyle rappers in the world, but she has made a career of being an American cultural ambassador, traveling from nation to nation, as a hiphop artist, crossing boundaries in the same way that American jazz musicians, for years, have done with the U.S. State Department.

Imagine if someone in Washington acknowledges our hiphop legends for their cultural contributions. It would be the path to truly honoring and recognizing a Kool Herc, an Afrika Bambaataa, a Grandmaster Flash, a Cold Crush Brothers, a Rock Steady Crew, a Universal Zulu Nation, an Ernie Paniciolli (the dean of hiphop photographers), and the numerous founding fathers and mothers of hiphop culture.

By treating them like the national treasures that they are—

Tyler Perry's "For Colored Girls"

NOVEMBER 2010
PUBLISHED IN DAILY KOS

Push pause before watching *for colored girls...*

People either love or hate filmmaker Tyler Perry—that much is clear to me. Weeks before I decided to see Perry's "For Colored Girls" on opening night I could hear the extreme reactions to the fact he was adapting, producing, and directing a film version of Ntozake Shange's classic 1970s choreopoem/play "For Colored Girls Who Have Considered Suicide When The Rainbow Is Enuf."

"I think Tyler is the worst filmmaker ever," one pal of mine said, an amazing actress and writer, who is completely traumatized that Perry was even permitted to touch Shange's writing.

And then there have been all the pre-film blogs written and passed around which have, in the main, been attempts to prepare viewers, particularly Black women movie goers, for the worst. Indeed, one blog I sampled encouraged women to read Shange's words first, to go as a group, almost as if bracing themselves for a natural disaster. Another blog demolished Perry as a proprietor of modern-day minstrel shows in real-time Black face. This woman's blog was so detailed in her point-by-point critiques of Tyler's pictures, that it set off what appears to be at least 100 responses, most supporting her views, with a few not, and a handful saying she was an extremist, and, better yet, a hater. And this last blog and its comments are from a year ago when it was first announced Perry was tackling Shange's piece.

(A not-so-humorous side note: From the hardcore reactions to one Tyler Perry, you would think his films have done as much damage to Black America as, say, racism, HIV/AIDS, failing public schools, rampant unemployment, crime, drug dealing and drug abuse, gentrification, the prison-industrial complex, police brutality, Republican right-wingers and the Fox News Channel, ghetto dictatorships and lazy leadership in the form of certain very identifiable Black politicians and Black preachers, corner liquor stores, fast food restaurants, and every other challenge you could name....)

Since then it hasn't helped that the trailer for the adaptation doesn't do the actual film any poetic justice. You see Janet Jackson far too much (it is clear Mr. Perry has an acute fascination with Ms. Jackson in spite of her well-meaning but limited acting abilities), and you see a plethora of quick-cut imagery in the film, but unless you've closely read the Shange book yourself, or have seen the words interpreted on the stage through the years, you come away from the trailer not really clear what the film narrative is.

As a result I was really torn about watching "For Colored Girls." First off, I have seen some of Perry's "Madea" films and, yes, they have made me cringe. How could they not when I know very well the history of Black images in America, how destructive so many of these images have been to our collective spirits, psyches, and bodies, be they mammy, big momma, tragic "mulatto," gangsta, thug, pimp, prostitute, thief, hustler, or bumbling, stumbling coon or buffoon. If there was a true and intentional balance to what we colored folks are given to digest on television, in movies, in music videos, in video games, and now on the internet, then there would hardly be a whisper about Tyler Perry's films. And if he had stayed in the urban Black theater scene—our theatrical version of the famous "chitlin' circuit" for Black performers—then no one, save poor or working-class and or church-going Black folks, would probably even know who Perry is today.

But it is precisely because those poor or working-class and or church-going Black folks flock to venues like the Beacon Theater in New York City, every time one of these plays is announced on local urban radio stations, that Tyler Perry is famous and fabulously wealthy. The plays are simplistic, but with enough Black around-the-way humor and morality lessons that serve as a necessary escape from the grind of our daily Black lives. Who would not want that? And is it little surprise that Perry's career first skyrocketed during the Bush II years, and continues to be an entertainment outlet for the souls of many Black folks during The Great Recession? No, he is not a great writer, not a great director, not a great actor. Not yet, and I have no clue if he will ever be any of those things. But Tyler Perry is an astute entrepreneur, a marketing genius, someone who has filled a huge void for working-class Black America, for church-going Black America, with film after film. Up until "For Colored Girls," Perry has not pretended to be an artist, or a super-talented director in the vein of Julie Dash, Martin Scorsese, or Kasi Lemmons.

No, what Perry has done is exactly what pioneering African American filmmaker Oscar Micheaux did from 1919 to 1948: give Black people themselves on screen on a regular basis, something that, as evidenced by Perry's huge box-office receipts with each film (including approximately $20 million this past opening weekend for "For Colored Girls"), we desperately crave. Indeed just as Oscar Micheaux steadily fed the Black masses with his 44 films and 7 novels (including one national bestseller) over those 29 years, Perry too has been relentless with his productivity and his work ethic, churning out, it feels, a film a year, if not two. This is on top of his plays, his television shows, and the running of his new state-of-the-art film and television studio in Georgia. But please be clear that Tyler Perry is not the first African American to own his own film and TV compound. No, that distinction belongs to Tim Reid and Daphne Maxwell Reid and what they built and opened in Virginia in the late 1990s. But Perry has taken the best of the hustle and flow of Micheaux, the bravado of Blaxploitation wonder-man Melvin Van Peebles, the make-Black-films-by-any-means-necessary mantra of Spike Lee, and the business savvy of the Reids, remixed the ingredients, and given us Tyler Perry, the baddest Black film mogul this side of the 21st century. And that begets a taste of power that makes Perry the Booker T. Washington of Black filmmakers. In other words, like how Booker T. was hotly debated in his day for his dealings with Black folks and issues of race, so too is Tyler P. hotly debated in his day for his dealings with Black folks and, yeah, issues of race (images).

But what one cannot deny about either is that in an America where it has always been extremely hard for Black folks to own and sustain institutions, both built institutions that stand as unbelievable achievements of the human spirit, and in spite of entrenched American racism and White privilege in the realms of education (Booker T.) and Hollywood (Tyler P.). One could even go so far as to say that outside of Oprah Winfrey, Perry is easily the most powerful Black entertainer in our nation, and one of the most influential regardless of race.

For Tyler Perry has taken the business of Black filmmaking to another level. A level that Micheaux, Van Peebles, and not even Spike Lee could have ever achieved. Because Tyler Perry is not only the master of his own ship, the owner of his vision and his brand, but he is now positioned to tackle Hollywood racism head on without ever uttering a single word about it. For sure, Perry says he does not discriminate against anyone, and that is clear from his diverse team of production folks. But it is also abundantly clear he has added brick after brick to the Spike Lee foundation of hiring Black people in every position possible, to nurture and train them for long careers in film and television production. The kind of opportunities they would not get elsewhere. I mean, when I look at the credits to, say, Francis Ford Coppola's epics, "The Godfather I and II," it is not lost on me the numerous Italian surnames. Coppola was clearly looking out for his people. So why can't Perry do the same for his?

But with the box office success, the full-fledged studio, the role as the most powerful Black person in Hollywood, and an uncanny ability to get every kind of Black actress or actor you can think of into his films (no matter the quality of the films), I imagine the question began to gnaw at Tyler as the refrain scrutinizing his filmmaking skills, or lack thereof, have grown louder and louder: Where do I, Tyler Perry, go from here?

Here, I believe, means Tyler knows, there in the underbelly of his Southern soul, that he cannot continue to make, solely, Madea films, preachy PG movies with one-dimensional characters and a gumbo pot full of plotlines. That he had to leave his comfort zone, had to create 34th Street Films so that he can begin to make more meaningful films, better developed and multi-faceted films, films written and directed by others, and perhaps others with extensive film training, who can bring to life the kind of Black tales seldom told, and seldom seen in the history of American cinema—

Push play: for colored girls unfolds....

Living in New York City for the past 20 years as both a writer and activist means I have seen and heard versions of Shange's choreopoem many many times. I even once lived with and dated an actress who, like many Black actresses, frequently used a monologue from "For Colored Girls..." in one audition or another. What I learned from my then-girlfriend, and from my Black female actress friends through the years, is that there is an enormous scarcity of monologues written specifically for Black women, that what Shange wrote really is as timeless as Shakespeare. And as poetic and lofty, too. That when you enter the world of Ntozake Shange's "For Colored Girls..." you are, in essence, entering high and sacred ground.

Which brings me back to my decision to see the film on opening night. The evening before I had visited my mother in my hometown of Jersey City, and there we were, in the same kitchen she has been in for 30-plus years. As I ate the fish my moms prepared for me, she sat, all 67 years of her, slightly slumped, in a plastic-covered chair by the stove. My mother looked both at peace, and well, very tired. Tired from years of being a Black woman in America. Tired from years of working in cotton fields, factories, and in the homes of the wealthy and the elderly. Tired of being tired, these several years later, from talking about how my father had wronged her. To the point, now, that she herself had aged with hints of sorrow in her heart and twinges of bitterness at the corners of her mouth. She, a colored girl, who had survived the hostile abandonment of my father, and all the would-be suitors who came to move in, not to love her. She, a colored girl, who had survived acute poverty, minimal life skills, and an 8th grade education to raise me, a Black boy, to be something other than yet another wretched statistic. Who will sing the coarse songs of women like my mother? Who will tell their tales if not us?

And then to the other extreme of why I was in Jersey City Thursday night: Judge Shirley Tolentino, the first Black woman judge I'd ever met, had died, and I went to St. Aloysius Church on Westside Avenue to pay my respects at her wake. And what a wake it was. The church was loaded with all kinds of people, mostly Black, there to say good-bye to a Black woman many considered one of Jersey's most powerful judges. I met her when I was a teen and driving my mother mad. I don't even recall what the particular indiscretion was with the law, but there I was in front of Judge Tolentino, utterly stunned a Black woman, this Black woman, was about to decide my fate. For whatever reason, she gave me a break, I never went to a juvenile detention center, never landed in jail, so I had to see her one last time, even in that coffin box, just to say "Thank you." I had thought of Judge Tolentino often through the years, long before I knew of Harriet Tubman or Sojourner Truth, or Ida B. Wells or Mary McLeod Bethune, or Shirley Chisholm or Angela Davis, or the ladies in Shange's "For Colored Girls...," or Michelle Obama, even. For Judge Tolentino, like my mother, represents a kind of power that Black women have always possessed, from the golden earth of Africa to the concrete jungles of America's inner cities, a power that said you may try to destroy us by all available means but like that Maya Angelou poem, still we rise—

And somewhere in Tyler Perry's life, ostensibly, he has been affected, aided, raised, prepared, by Black women like the ones I know. All us Black boys know them. No, I have not always liked the way Perry has depicted Black women in his films, but I also cannot ignore how many Black actresses he has employed, quite a few of them so remarkably gifted by their God yet so completely shunned or forgotten by Hollywood. Nor can I disregard that in his newly minted studio are soundstages named after Black female acting giants like Ruby Dee and Cicely Tyson. Somewhere in Perry croons an undying love for Black women—

Yes, these things were on my mind as I made my way to the Brooklyn Academy of Music to see Perry's film. I purposely sat in the back row so that I could watch any who entered. And here they came, slowly but surely, Black women like my mother, and Black women like Judge Tolentino. Younger Black women and older Black women. Straight Black women and lesbian or bisexual Black women. Black women with perms and weaves, and Black women with dreadlocks or baldheads. There were a few of us Black males present, and a few White sisters and brothers. I could feel some Black female eyes on me as I sat alone, wondering what had brought me to this film, maybe. I think if I had suffered through what countless Black women have suffered through in their lives, including my mother, I would question, too. For what is it to live in a nation where you have been victimized not only because of your race, but also because of your sex? Where you have not only had to contend with sheer madness ranging from slave masters to corporate bosses with a reckless disregard for your being, but also from husbands, boyfriends, lovers, fathers, grandfathers, uncles, sons, and grandsons whose own internalized racism and oppression have destroyed them and, in effect, destroyed you. This is the heaviness of experience and history that these Black women march with into one Tyler Perry movie after another. They simply want to see fragments of themselves on screen, be it Madea or Shange's "For Colored Girls." And most of these women are not like my actress friends, not like my cultural critics friends, not like my academic or scholarly friends, and not like my bohemian friends: well versed in all things Black, cultural, artistic, political, or literary. They are more like my mother, a woman who does not read books, save bits and pieces of the bible, and who has never really been told (nor mustered the strength to tell herself) that she is beautiful, that she is powerful, that she is visible. Which is why since the 1970s when I was a child, as far back as I can remember, my mother mostly goes to the movies when it is Black people up on the screen. My moms is especially fond of Whoopi Goldberg and I suspect it is because Whoopi, like my mother, is a dark-complexioned Black woman who has been told, more times than not, that she is ugly, and you and I both know that Whoopi, and my mother, are quite beautiful. Therefore in seeing Whoopi shine on that screen my mother is seeing herself shine, is seeing her beautiful brown skin shine in a way it never shined in those cotton fields, in those factories, in the homes of those wealthy or elderly folks, and certainly never shined in the eyes of my long-gone father. Women like my mother, younger and older, simply need to know that their lives are valid, that their lives do matter. Love him or hate him, that is the space Tyler Perry has created for many a Black person, a space my mother asked me to share with her when she requested "Can you take me to see that movie about them colored girls?" Yes, ma, I will—

So there is this film, and as "For Colored Girls" began, I washed away the negative reviews I'd read, the questions on why him to do this, and simply watched the movie. I would say about 15 minutes into it I realized I was watching something very different than other Perry flicks, that he had grown as a filmmaker, that he was not butchering Shange's words as so many had suggested he would, or had.

Instead what we were getting was a 21st century reading of "For Colored Girls," very much required, in reality, given that Shange's piece was created in the 1970s. And no different, undoubtedly, than Ethan Hawke taking Shakespeare's "Hamlet" and setting it at the Denmark Corporation in his early 2000s film version, while retaining the old language. If Hawke could keep the old language and update the setting, why can't Perry? Moreover, it was clear to me, as the drama unfolded, that many in the theater, including the Black woman sitting right next to me, had never read the Shange book, nor had ever seen a staged production. Tyler Perry's flick was it, was their introduction. And in this world of fast-paced videos, Twitter, and every manner of cell phone with video components, Perry has taken the best of what Shange has willed to us, combined it with a stellar ensemble that features Phylicia Rashad, Whoopi Goldberg, Anika Noni Rose, Kimberly Elise, Thandie Newton, and Loretta Devine, and created something that is, well, very special and quite magical, in spite of the hurt and pain peppered throughout this film.

The film had to be given a bona fide backdrop in Harlem, the men had to be given some voices here and there, and the women's names could not merely be Lady in Red, Lady in Brown, and so on. We need to know them as Crystal and Yasmine and Jo. Need to know their names because those names are the real names of real Black women who live in Harlem, Brooklyn, Oakland,

Los Angeles, Chicago, Detroit, Atlanta, D.C., St. Louis, Houston, wherever Black women be. But Perry had to cast his bucket somewhere, so Harlem became the metaphor for anywhere America, specifically one walk-up apartment building where most of the characters dwell. Think of how Gloria Naylor put her main female characters on one block in her majestic novel "The Women of Brewster Place." Or how a Brooklyn neighborhood exploded off the screen in Spike's "Do The Right Thing." With "For Colored Girls" I was awestruck by the color palettes used for the film, the exquisiteness of these Black women's many skin hues, the imaginative method in which Perry stitched Shange's original words in with freshly written lines to make the narrative go. And go they do, for they are brilliant, hardworking, dedicated, steadfast, loving, divine, and, often, very very lonely in their own skins. You feel it with Phylicia Rashad's character, the manager of the building, whose sole purpose at this moment seems to be as ears and eyes of what is happening with her neighbors. But it is in helping them through their pain that gives her life a pulse. You feel it in Whoopi Goldberg's character, so terrified of the universe that she has turned her apartment into a shrine of boxes filled with God only knows what, her life reduced to prayers, prayer oils, and an overwhelming belief that anyone who does not believe in her God and her religion is destined for hell, including her two daughters. You feel it in the innocence of Anika Noni Rose's character, wide-eyed and recently out of a relationship, and so horrifically duped by a handsome man into a rape scene and subsequent monologue that was so jarring it felt like the entire theater had instantly become a mountainous chorus of tears, wails, and gasps for air. And you feel it in Kimberly Elise, so broken by mental abuse and domestic violence that she is just one step from a complete nervous breakdown. And then her husband does it, he murders her two children in broad daylight, dropping them—and the sanity and heart of Elise's character— from their apartment window, their blood smeared on the asphalt below like the jagged journey of Black women and girls in America.

"I never thought I'd see the day when I enjoyed a Tyler Perry film," said one female friend, and I concurred with her. But I am not sure if "enjoy" is the right word. "For Colored Girls" is a conversation, a mirror, something, obviously, that one culturally and socially ignorant film critic after another just did not get as they blasted the film in their reviews. One repeated critique is that the movie deals too much in pathologies. Are you going to tell me that Coppola's "Godfather I and II," widely hailed as two of the best movies of all time, are not riddled with multiple social pathologies? Likewise with "Citizen Kane," or "Forrest Gump," even? So to these over-the-top haters of Perry's "For Colored Girls," What film, exactly, were you watching that that is the sum of what you viewed? How does one come away from that film and not agree that Kimberly Elise should be nominated for a Best Actress Oscar, and Thandie Newton (with Anika Noni Rose and Whoopi Goldberg not far behind) for a Best Supporting Actress Oscar? How does one not acknowledge the terrific score, the captivating cinematography, or the set design, even? And how does one gripe that the back-alley abortion scene is not credible in these times if one has never been to, never lived in, nor ever spent significant time in an American ghetto and, as a consequence, is not fully aware of the physical and psychological lengths us poor Black folks have historically had to go to, even in the age of Obama and in an allegedly post-racial America, to duck and dodge the slings and arrows of outrageous fortune?

Additionally, I do know if a Tom Hanks, a man who was on a mediocre television sitcom and made mediocre film after mediocre film in the 1980s, could reinvent himself as a leading man and Oscar winner in the 1990s, then why can't Tyler Perry be given the space to evolve, to grow, to be something other than what first made his fame and fortune? Or if a Marvin Gaye could go from crooning catchy but clichéd Motown pop ballads to making a masterpiece model for social protest music with "What's Going On?" then why can't we believe, in our hearts, that Perry made a strong, compelling, and emotionally-riveting movie with "For Colored Girls?"

Yes, there are flaws in the film. Here are the glaring ones for me: Janet Jackson, who I have always loved in general, just should not be in the film nor should she have been given top billing. Janet simply does not have the range and depth she displayed as a child actor on "Good Times." Next, the director did not push Kerry Washington hard enough, I feel, to display the kind of emotional dexterity needed for her character as she witnessed the breaking down of lives about her, and her inability to have a baby. And it was so pathetically predictable that Janet's husband in the film would turn out to be "a brother on the down-low." We've got to stop fanning the flames of fear and homophobia to Black people like that, once and for all. The issue with HIV/AIDS in Black America is sexual dishonesty and sexual irresponsibility across the board, not whether someone is straight or gay. Everyone has to be more honest and everyone has to be more careful. That scene is one moment of a few in the film where I felt we were getting the old Tyler Perry, the Perry as Madea film where the script got stiff and, well, lethargic and unimaginative.

And, no, for the record, I as a Black man had no problem whatsoever with the depiction of Black males in the film. "For Colored Girls" is not a male-bashing film. It is a story about women and if you, a man, happen to be uncomfortable with what you see and hear, then maybe it is because elements of who you be are in some of those characters. I absolutely thought about my own relationships with Black women through the years as I digested "For Colored Girls," thought of women I have dated, women I have treated correctly and as my equals, and of women I've treated poorly or disrespectfully. So if you are an honest man, one serious about your own growth and evolution, then you come to "For Colored Girls," or any story about women and girls, with emotional courage and integrity, not disdain, finger-pointing, and haterism.

Unfortunately, this same wave of negative male responses occurred when Shange's "For Colored Girls..." opened on Broadway in the 1970s, and with "The Color Purple," the film, in the mid1980s. So it is to be expected given the patriarchy, sexism, and misogyny that runs rampant on our planet, still. Men will refuse to see the film and say it is unfair to them just because. But what is missing is that we males do need to listen to the stories of women, do need to empathize with their highs and their lows, do need to understand how much more we can learn about ourselves, if we simply develop the intellectual muscle to listen to the blues songs of women, including the women who are our mothers, grandmothers, sisters, aunts, nieces, cousins, lovers, bosses, employees, wives, friends—

But, alas, in an American society as drenched in sexism as it is in racism, that is a huge leap for many of us. Male privilege is a tough thing to shake, above all when we've been conditioned our entire lives to believe we are the superior sex, to believe that the only way to view the world is through our eyes. As if the women's eyes don't matter at all. The stories told in "For Colored Girls" are very factual, happen to women in Black, White, Latina, Asian, and Native American communities every single day; happen to women who are Christian, Jewish, Muslim, and other faiths, or no faiths whatsoever; and those stories, in particular the ones of rape and domestic violence, are the reasons why it was stated in a *New York Times Magazine* article in 2009 that global violence against women is the human rights issue of the 21st century.

What that means, matter of fact, for my community, the Black community, is that we've got some long-held and far-rooted traumas that we've got to deal with immediately. That was evident from the excessive laughter during scenes that were clearly not funny. Also evident by all the Black folks complaining about the audience chatter that took place during their viewing of the film. Or complaints of cell phones that went off. Mad annoying and each gripe valid, yes, but worthy of long Facebook posts and blistering denigration of each other that reeks of Black self-hatred and, in some cases, blatant classism by some of my more, uh, uppity and uptight Black sisters and brothers? No. But as long as we continue to suffer from what scholars and activists in Black America refer to as "post-traumatic slave syndrome," passed from generation to generation, like a baton in a relay race, where your pain becomes your child's pain, and so on and so forth, then we will continue to be divided, inwardly and outwardly. Was that not clear from the scarred and shredded relationship between the characters depicted by Whoopi Goldberg and Thandie Newton? At the end of the day, people who are hurting simply want love, but often fail to recognize the first love must be of self. In sexing all those men in the film, Newton's character was essentially ducking and dodging the inner her, and ducking and dodging the past she needed to confront, finally. That is why that coming together of community at the end of "For Colored Girls" is so critical, and so necessary. For none of us can go it alone. Yes, Black males have issues too and, and yes, we deserve films that present us as whole human beings, as well, but that is not the point of "For Colored Girls," nor should it be; and, no, Black women are not abandoning us simply because of one film, but Perry's "For Colored Girls" does suggest that if we are to be healthy, and whole, then it means we've got to make conscious decisions to come together in a way where I am not hurting you and you are not hurting me. And to love our powerful and beautiful selves before it is too late— That is the challenge for Mr. Tyler Perry, as "For Colored Girls" continues to make money and continues to be both debated and disparaged. That is, can Tyler Perry—or will Tyler Perry—strive and struggle to transform the one-man economy his films have manifested, and use his voice, and his power, to push the envelope to make films, Black films, that not only show the vast complexities of the Black experience in America, and on this planet, but to also be spaces, simply by virtue of the genius of the work he produces and endorses for others, that can be healing circles for as many of us as possible? Will Perry, the next time a woman's story is presented to him, step aside and support a dynamic Black female director like Nzingha Stewart, Julie Dash, Ayoka Chenzira, or Kasi Lemmons? Will he, as a man, use his male privilege to make sure, in fact, that "For Colored Girls" the movie is not the last time, for decades and decades, we see such rich and layered depictions of Black women in theaters? Tall orders, yes, but I don't think Perry has been given this grand opportunity just for the sake of making dollars. As Perry admitted himself in one interview, he tried to avoid doing "For Colored Girls," both on Broadway and on film, but it kept coming back to him. Now it is done, it is out, and it is what he does from this moment forward that will determine his place in cinematic history and whether Tyler Perry's body of work will ultimately be a legacy for the ages.

Guns in America

JANUARY 2011
PUBLISHED IN DAILY KOS

"Annie Christian was a whore always looking for some fun
being good was such a bore, so she bought a gun
she killed John Lennon, shot him down cold
she tried to kill Reagan, everybody say gun control"
- *Prince, "Annie Christian" (1981)*

"...a prayer vigil/press conference at Brookdale Hospital
to pray for the 16 year old girl that was shot point blank in
the face. The Saturday, January 15th shooting took place on
Belmont and Sackman in Brownsville, Brooklyn...."
- *Email posted by Brooklyn clergy/community leaders (2011)*

Prince, the musical genius and icon, was singing about an
American mindset of 30 long years ago, one that is very alive
today. And, obviously, far more males than females engage in
gunplay as evidenced by who shot John Lennon, President Ronald
Reagan, and Congresswoman Gabrielle Giffords. Regardless of
the metaphors, we should heed Prince's point.

And the Brooklyn girl referenced above is Kervina Ervin, who was in critical condition but has progressed enough that she will now have surgery on her mouth, since it was badly damaged by the bullet. There has been much speculation on why Kervina was shot (Was it gang-related? Was it revenge for some prior street fight?). But what is clear is that Kervina is, symbolically, millions of miles away from Tucson, Arizona, and the national outpouring of grief (well-deserved) that has accompanied the day-to-day vigil for Congresswoman Giffords.

For sure, Kervina Ervin's life is as valuable as the Congresswoman's. Yet we would not know that because there has been no presidential visit to Brownsville, one of the poorest communities in America, and a 'hood whose pockmarked skies are often littered with the pop pop pop of bullets.

Nor has there been round-the-clock media coverage. What we have instead is Kervina's family, led by her mother, doing the best they can to make sure Kervina survives that gunshot.

And I wish I could say Kervina was the sole victim of gun violence in Brooklyn in January, but I cannot. For the period of Friday, January 14, 2011, through Thursday, January 20, 2011, there were 2 murders, 7 non-fatal shooting incidents, with a total of 11 non-fatal shooting victims. And that is only for communities in northern Brooklyn. Imagine what is happening in other parts of this New York City borough that I love dearly, or in so-called ghettoes nationwide. Right here in our America we are losing a generation of young people to gun blasts that rival the violence in Afghanistan or Iraq, or in other war-torn countries.

Accordingly, as we debate guns, gun control, and what happened, precisely, in Tucson, Arizona on Saturday, January 8th, and who, exactly, is responsible, I think it time we cease pointing fingers at each other and take a good look in the mirror at ourselves.

For there is something wrong with us as a people, as Americans, when some of us can justify, in the aftermath of that Arizona shooting tragedy, or the countless shootings in America's suburbs and inner cities, the right to bear arms. I am very clear what the Second Amendment says but, honestly, it is tough to hear those words this very moment, especially since I have had to deliver eulogies at more funerals than I can count. And console more mothers, fathers, relatives, friends, and distraught community members than I care to recollect. Each and every single funeral tied to gun violence.

For that reason America needs to be completely transparent about the fact that we have a profound and dysfunctional relationship with guns, that we are literally blowing each other away, and few seem genuine in their desire to stop the bloodshed for good.

For sure, as I sat in my living room during our most recent Dr. Martin Luther King holiday weekend, gunshots spit from the bowels of Fort Greene Projects, directly across the street from my condo building. I could not help but think of the great irony of the hate email I had received since the Arizona shooting tragedy. Individuals saying I had incredible nerve to call for gun control, that I was "un-American," "unpatriotic," and one critic essentially figured out a way to portray me as anti- our American soldiers overseas because of my desire for major gun control.

I also hear the words, frequently, of what my dear friend April Silver said to me in the aftermath of Congresswoman Giffords being shot: "Kev, you are out there as a public figure, too. That could have been you—"

It could have been any of us with strong opinions about our nation and our world that someone out there does not like. But I am not afraid, and I am not anti- anything. I am for nonviolence, love, respect, and peaceful solutions to conflicts. And I want to stop the endless merry-go-round of Americans, regardless of background, being wounded, maimed, paralyzed, or murdered purely because someone figures the only way to resolve a beef or differing point of view is through the barrel of a gun.

Indeed, when something like the Arizona calamity happens, or the mass killing on the campus of Virginia Tech (2007), or the slaughter at the Fort Hood military base in Texas (2009), or the Columbine High School shooting in Colorado (1999), we Americans are aghast with horror, we freeze, we ponder and reflect, and vow, with substantial passion, that we will not allow this to happen again. And then it does. At our homes, at our workplaces or our schools, on our public transportation systems. Wherever we be, there be bullets flying when we least expect it.

Just this past weekend, in fact, we had the shooting outside a Washington State Walmart that left two dead and two Sheriff's deputies wounded. Both the shooter and a teenaged girl police believe was somehow connected to the suspect were killed. In Detroit, a lone gunman was brazen enough to walk into a police precinct, opened fire, and wounded four officers before return gunfire took his life.

Why? Because we are a violent nation, a nation that was founded on violence. Just ask Native Americans, Black Americans who had to trek through slavery and segregation, poor and or ethnic Whites, Mexicans, women, the LGBT community, or any other group in our lengthy and hectic history who have had to deal with guns being aimed in their direction. No question that we are a nation that has often settled scores, in our wars, in our movies, in our video games, and, no doubt, in our political gripes, with gunplay. Or with talk or boasts of gunplay. Pump that, like a drug, into the minds and veins of any people enough, and add anger, rage, alienation, or, yes, emotional instability or mental illness, and you've got a recipe for American tragedy after American tragedy.

That said, the great misfortune to me is not simply Tucson, Arizona. God bless those victims and survivors, and God knows I am praying for Congresswoman Giffords' full recovery. But the greater misfortunes are the ignored, forgotten, or anonymous individuals, like Kervina Ervin, who wonder, each and every single day of their lives, in some cases, if they will catch a bullet, as we say, just because they live in a community where guns are so easy to obtain. Or if they are the wife or girlfriend of a man who is an abuser and has threatened to shoot them. And the stories go on and on—

That is why stats like these are so staggering:

1) Since 1968, when Dr. King and Robert F. Kennedy were murdered, with guns, over a million Americans have been killed, with guns

2) In any given year there are over 9000 gun-related murders in America. In developed nations like England there is 39 per year, or just 17 in Finland in any given year

3) Murder rates due to guns in America are 6.9 times the rates in 22 other heavily populated and high-income countries combined

4) Medical costs and costs to the criminal justice system, in America, plus all the security precautions (think of metal detectors at airports, at schools, and elsewhere) wind up costing us, as taxpayers, over $100 billion per year

What we are discussing, then, is a national crisis that must become a national priority and a national conversation, led by our president, Barack Obama. Mr. Obama should start by urging passage of a bill, H.R. 308, to ban large capacity ammunition magazines, an important life-saving measure now before Congress.

Beyond this, under President Obama's leadership we as citizens sick and tired of being sick and tired of gun violence need to challenge our elected officials to put more meat on the

Brady Bill, signed into law by President Clinton in the 1990s. That means cities, towns, states, and the national government have got to work together to make it much more difficult to get a gun. We've got to fix the background check system immediately, create a national formula for that, and make all records available of anyone who wants to purchase a gun, including medical and criminal records, or any reports from a school or workplace of unstable behavior. And those loopholes that make it so easy to get a gun without any check whatsoever must be closed. What kind of nation are we that a teenager, or even younger, can presently get a gun from someone, and use it for deadly purposes, as if he, or she, were playing a video game for fun?

When I look at how easily Jared Lee Loughner was able to secure a weapon to shoot Congresswoman Giffords and others, I just scratch my head and wonder where were the background checks, the sharing of information about his emotional instability and why, for God's sake, was he pulled over by the police, just moments before the tragedy, and summarily allowed to carry on?

(The running joke in many Black communities, and not so funny, either, is that if Mr. Loughner were Black, no way the police would have allowed him to carry on so easily. Well....)

I am not suggesting that any one individual or institution is responsible, but certainly we are in this together. That means some of us have got to get the courage to stand up to the National Rifle Association, finally, and to gun manufacturers. And to gun sellers as well, be they at gun shows, or in the streets, back alleys, or hallways of America. It is a kind of national sickness to think it normal to carry a gun, to have access to a gun, just because you want one. But, conversely, when I was speaking at a college in rural Maryland last weekend, a student asked me about guns for those who hunt for food. I had to pause for a second and recall that my own South Carolina born and bred family (although I am personally a vegan these days) hunted to survive. And that some of my kinfolk, in the South, still do. Until we have an alternative way of feeding every single American, I can't be mad at folks for doing that, even if I don't personally like it. There is a big difference between hunting for survival's sake and hunting people, like prey, just because—

But what I am also concerned about is a gun lobby so powerful that fought, tooth and nail, against the Brady Bill, and which continues to jump through those loopholes that make gun access so easy. We the American people must collectively gather the nerve to challenge these folks until they, and we, understand that we do not need "civility," as has been argued since the Arizona tragedy.

No, what we need is a culture of nonviolence, one where, again, it becomes a national priority right in pre-school or grade school, to teach our children the lessons of Gandhi, of Dr. King, of anyone who is rationale enough to understand violence in any form, or the ready availability of guns, is simply not acceptable for a society that calls itself civilized.

And this conversation is not just for everyday American citizens, either. It needs to extend to some in law enforcement who are what the singer Marvin Gaye once crooned, "trigger-happy polices," especially given the rampant use of gunfire at

Black and Latino males in our urban environments. Yes, being a police officer is a dangerous job and I have the utmost respect for our police forces. But they too have been contaminated by a culture of violence where brute force, or gunshots, has often become the first and only solution for our conflicts, problems, or fears.

Thus if we are going to talk about guns and gun violence, the national conversation must be from every single angle. Each one of us must ask ourselves why is it okay to reside in a culture where violent blockbuster movies rule our theaters, why television habitually features gunplay, why historical tales we've digested since childhood have always featured weapons and violence, and why it is okay for our children, or us, too, to play video games that showcase violent imagery that feed our seemingly insatiable appetites for murder and mayhem, even if it is fictionalized?

This is the only way we as a nation will turn this corner, if we are totally real with ourselves, and are willing to steer the DNA of our culture in a new direction. And as Martin Luther King III said earlier today, at a press conference with New York City Mayor Michael Bloomberg in response to the crisis of guns in America,

"We are a much better nation than the behavior exhibited."

And way past time for us to show it. For our children. And our children's children, too—

Joe Paterno, Herman Cain, Men, Sex, and Power

NOVEMBER 2011
PUBLISHED IN DAILY KOS

Joe Paterno. Herman Cain. Penn State football. Presidential campaigns. Men. Sex. Power. Women. Harassed. Children. Abused.

These are some of the hash tags that have tweeted through my mind nonstop, these past several days, as multiple sexual harassment charges have been hurled at Republican presidential candidate Herman Cain; as Jerry Sandusky, former defensive coordinator for Penn State's storied football program, was arrested on 40 counts related to allegations of sexual abuse of eight young boys over a 15-year period. Sandusky's alleged indiscretions have not only brought back very ugly and unsettling memories of the Catholic Church sexual abuse mania a few short years ago, but has led to the firing of legendary coach Joe Paterno and Penn State president Graham Spanier, plus the indictments of athletic director Tim Curley and a vice president, Gary Schultz, for failing to report a grad assistant's eyewitness account of Sandusky allegedly having anal sex with a ten-year-old boy in a shower on the university's campus in 2002.

In the matter of Mr. Herman Cain I cringed, to be blunt, as I watched his press conference this week denying accusations of sexual harassment against him, which has swelled to four different women, two identified and two anonymous, for now. I was not there, so I don't know, only he and the women know the truth. But what was telling in Mr. Cain's remarks is that he was visibly defensive and defiant, rambled quite a bit about the media's smear campaign and, most curious, only once mentioned sexual harassment as a major problem in America, and it was just one quick, passing sentence. Then he went back to discussing himself, which he is particularly adept at doing.

What Herman Cain and the disgraced male leaders of Penn State have in common is the issue of power and privilege we men not only wield like our birthright, but which has come to be so inextricably linked to our identities. So much so, in fact, that many of us, regardless of race, class, religion and, in some cases, even sexual orientation or physical abilities, don't even realize what a disaster manhood is when it is unapologetically invested in power, privilege, patriarchy, sexism, and a reckless disregard for the safety and sanity of others, especially women and children.

Every single year, it seems, some well-known man somewhere gets into trouble because of sex, money, drugs, or violence, or some combination thereof (and God only knows how many unknown males do likewise). It is always the same themes, just with a new cast of characters. Yesterday it was priests of the Catholic Church. Today it is the male leadership of Penn State. Yesterday it was Anthony Weiner and Charlie Sheen. Today it is Herman Cain. I remember earlier this year, in fact, in the wake of Mr. Weiner's sudden and rapid fall from grace, a report was published that said over 90 percent of sex scandals in America feature us men as the culprits. That very few women engage in that mode of self-destructive behavior. The question begs itself: Why not? I feel it has to do with how we construct manhood from birth. Most of us boys are taught, basically from the time we can talk and walk, to be strong, tough, loud, dominating, aggressive, and, yes, even violent, even if that violence is masked in tales of war or Saturday afternoon college football games. Without anything to counteract that mindset like, say, that it is okay for boys and men to tell the truth, to show raw emotions and vulnerability, to cry, to view girls and women as our equals on every level, we are left with so many of us, far into adulthood, as fully formed physically but incredibly undeveloped emotionally. And if you are a male who happens to have been sexually assaulted or abused yourself, and never got any real help in any form, highly likely you will at some point become a sexual predator yourself. And if you are a man who still thinks we are in pre-feminist movement America where it was once okay to, well, touch, massage, or caress a female colleague inappropriately, to talk sex to her, as she is either working for you or attempting to secure a job (and has not given you permission to do so), then you are also likely to be the kind of male who will deny any of it ever happened. Again and again and again—

The bottom line is that our notions of manhood are totally

and embarrassingly out of control, and some of us have got to stand up and say enough, that we've got to redefine what it is to be a man, even as we, myself included, are unfailingly forthright about our shortcomings and our failures as men, and how some of us have even engaged in the behaviors splashed across the national news this year alone.

But to get to that new kind of manhood means we've got to really dig into our souls and admit the old ways are not only not working, but they are so painfully hurtful to women, to children, to communities, businesses, institutions, and government, to sport and play, and to ourselves. Looking in the mirror is never easy but if not now, when? And if not us in these times, then we can surely expect the vicious cycles of manhood gone mad to continue for generations to come, as evidenced by a recent report in the New York Times of a steadily climbing number of American teen boys already engaging in lewd sexual conduct toward girls. Where are these boys learning these attitudes if not from the men around them, in person, in the media, on television and in film, in video games, or from their fathers, grandfathers, uncles, older brothers, teachers, and, yes, coaches? For sure, nothing sadder and more tragic than to see 84-year-old Coach Joe Paterno, who I've admired since I was a child, throwing away 46 years of coaching heroism and worship (and 62 total years on the school's football staff) because the power, glory, and symbolism of Penn State football was above protecting the boys allegedly touched and molested by Sandusky. Equally sad and tragic when Mr. Cain's supporters are quick to call what is happening to him a lynching when this man, this Black man, has never been tarred and feathered, never been hung from a tree, never had his testicles cut from his body, never been set on fire, as many Black men were, in America, in the days when lynching was as big a national sport as college football is today. Anything, it seems, to refute the very graphic and detailed stories of the women accusing Mr. Cain of profoundly wrong, unprofessional, and inhuman conduct.

But, as I stated, when our sense of manhood has gone mad, completely mad, anything goes, and anything will be said (or nothing said at all), or done, to protect the guilty, at the expense of the innocent. We've got to do better than this, gentlemen, brothers, boys, for the sake of ourselves, for the sake of our nation and our world. It was Albert Einstein who famously stated that insanity is doing the same thing over and over and expecting a different result. Then insanity may also mean men and boys doing the same things over and over again, for the sake of warped and damaged manhood, and expecting forward progress to happen, but then it all crumbles, once more, in a heap of facts, finger-pointing, and forgetful memories when convenient.

If any good can come of the Cain and Penn State disasters it is my sincere hope that spaces and movements are created, finally, where we men can really begin to rethink what manhood can be, what manhood might be. Manhood that is not about power, privilege, and the almighty penis, but instead rooted in a sense of humanity, in peace, in love, in nonviolence, in honesty and transparency, in constant self-criticism and self-reflection, and in respect and honor of women and girls, again, as our equals; in spaces and movements where men and boys who might not be hyper-macho and sports fanatics like some us are not treated as outcasts, as freaks, as less than men or boys. A manhood where if we see something bad happening, we say something, and not simply stick our heads in the sand and pretend that something did not happen. Or worse, yet, do something wrong ourselves, and when confronted with that wrongness, rather than confess, acknowledge, grow, heal, evolve, we instead dig in our heels and imagine ourselves in an all-out war, proclaiming our innocence to any who will listen, even as truth grows, like tall and daunting trees in a distant and darkened woods, about us.

A manhood, alas, where we men and boys understand that we must be allies to women and girls, allies to all children, and be much louder, visible, and outspoken about sexual harassment, rape, domestic violence, sexual abuse and molestation. Knowing that if we are on the frontlines of these human tragedies then we can surely help to make them end once and for all, for the good of us all.

That means time for some of us to grow, and to grow up. Time for some of us to let go of the ego trips and the pissing contests to protect bruised and battered egos of boys masquerading as men. Before it is too late, before some of us hurt more women, more children, and more of ourselves, yet again—

PART **TWO**

Like A Rolling Stone...

Kevin Powell's financial life. And yours, too.

AUGUST 2010
PUBLISHED IN HUFFINGTON POST

"And ye shall know the truth, and the truth shall make you free."
- *John 8:32*

When I was a child, my mother would regularly quote that line from the book of John in the Bible about the truth setting us free. For ours was a very harsh life, as my grade school-educated mother was forced to raise me alone, after my father just disappeared (they were never married). There were years and years of welfare, food stamps, government cheese, and the kind of poverty I would not wish on anyone. In spite of these circumstances, my mother always encouraged me to work hard, to be honest at all times, and to keep God first in my life. Yet like most people in America struggling from paycheck to paycheck, there was little to no savings, no investments, no assets, and we never knew of anything in the way of financial literacy or empowerment workshops. My mother simply took the coins and dollar bills she had and made magic happen year to year. One of my most vivid memories of my childhood is my mother and I going with my mother to the local deli and getting baloney, going with my mother always nudging the butcher "to slice it a little thicker, please." It was her way of saying "We do not have any money, and I need this baloney to last as long as possible."

The other thing I remember about my mother and finances is that she was always preaching to me "Save your money" as I held down several jobs in my adolescence, including newspaper routes, delivering groceries, and those low-paying and long-hours summer jobs for the city. But it is one thing to tell someone to "Save your money," and another to actually show them how. Perhaps because my mother worked so hard to make ends meet, and perhaps because she simply did not have the formal education to teach me, fully, how to be financially wise, even with no resources, I simply never got that lesson until many, many years later.

So in 2010, as I run for Congress here in Brooklyn, New York City's largest borough, and I am being attacked by my opponent and some in the media for having financial debt and owing taxes, I felt now was the appropriate time to come forth about my financial life. Anyone who truly knows me, or has followed my work for years—as a community leader, as a writer, as a public speaker, or has seen me on television programs like "Oprah"—knows that all Kevin Powell has ever been is honest and transparent. That will never change because we have far too many people in the world, particularly in politics, who are absolute and unapologetic liars.

The above said, having debt, struggling to pay one's mortgage or rent, or owing taxes does not make you a bad person. It makes you a regular person, one of millions and millions of Americans who are in similar situations regardless of race, class, gender, religion, sexual orientation, or geography. This, in fact, is one of the reasons why I decided to run for Congress again in 2010, after my first real bid in 2008. I am not going to lie. That previous race not only left me in financial debt, but it was coupled with the recession literally stopping cold my main source of income, delivering speeches at colleges and universities.

As a matter of fact, 2009 turned out to be the worst financial year of my life and it was not pleasant being dragged into court to deal with a mortgage and the need for a loan modification program. Nor was it fun to watch friends, colleagues, and neighbors around me lose their homes or jobs or both, forfeit their apartments, or suddenly find themselves on government assistance programs. I imagined a similar fate for myself, but I managed to get through 2009, by the grace of God and the kindness of quite a few friends.

Consequently I decided to run for Congress again, in spite of my own difficult financial situation a year ago, because I care so much for the community. Person after person shared their financial struggles with me, and person after person asked me to give it another shot, to win not just for me but for all the folks like us who are dealing with everyday challenges my opponent could not fathom. I knew I would be scrutinized much harder this time around. I knew there would be questions about every single aspect of my life. But leadership often means great sacrifices and a kind of nakedness of one's soul that most would never want to encounter. And, frankly, given what I have experienced on this very public stage the past few years, I really don't blame them. But I've chosen this as my life work, helping people to help themselves, so I really have no other choice, in spite of my own personal struggles. What our nation needs, more than ever, are jobs, better public education, and community healing on various fronts, and I feel my life journey and my twenty-plus years as an activist and agent for social issues position me to help and understand everyday people in a way my opponent just does not after 27 long and uneventful years in Congress.

So, yes, again, of course I have debt, lots of it. It really began when I left my mother's house at age 18 for college on a financial aid package, 26 years ago. Four years later I was kicked out of college, never finished, and all I had to show for it was a mountain of student loans and the prompting of my mother to "go get a job." Which I did, but with my eyes firmly on fulfilling my childhood dream of being a writer. Within a few years, due to a lot of persistence and a great deal of luck, I had appeared on the very first season of MTV's landmark reality show "The Real World," and also became a staff writer for Quincy Jones' *Vibe* magazine. Literally overnight I had gone from the poor ghetto child who had been tossed from college to a 20something and very well-known writer for America's fastest growing publication. But underneath that celebrity gloss were some very serious realities:

One, we were paid approximately only $2000 and no future royalties at all for "The Real World." And, yes, I did make good money working at *Vibe*, but like most young people who were never taught basic financial responsibility beyond "Save your money," I blew through it in the four years I was affiliated with that publication; and when my career there was over, what I had to show for it was a stereo system and a computer. It's like I had never been paid at all.

And once my relationship with *Vibe* soured in 1996, I plunged into an alcoholic-fueled depression for the remainder of the 1990s, not paying much attention to my finances, and allowing a hack accountant to know more about my financial life than I did.

Two decisions with very different results came of that critical period in my life. First I decided to quit journalism and the entertainment industry entirely, and to devote my life to activism, as I had done in my earlier years, back during college. Second, I felt so badly burned by my first accountant that I did not retain another one for several years. The great part of these decisions is that I made public speaking my main source of income and was able to visit nearly all 50 states in our country over time, and I cannot tell you how much traveling and interacting with so many different types of Americans profoundly changed my life, and cemented my desire to be help people, all people, for the rest of my life.

The downside of these decisions is that the more I became involved in community work in New York City and elsewhere (I did extensive Hurricane Katrina relief work, for example), the less interested I became in money and material things. I sacrificed everything to help strangers, family members, anyone who asked for my assistance. As long as I had a place to live, food to eat, and clothes to wear, I was good. Even during my

Vibe days, I never was about material things. For sure, to this very day I have never owned an automobile, and have never worn much jewelry beyond a basic watch. In spite of all I have experienced in the past 20 years alone, I remain very much that person who grew up with little to nothing. A shock to many because of whatever celebrity they think I have, but what they fail to realize is that I have no real interest in that lifestyle. I did, for a moment in the 1990s, but that moment is gone and what I do now is what matters to me.

Thus what wound up happening is the neglect of my finances in the 1990s became exacerbated in much of the 2000s by my intense desire to serve people more than take care of myself. A foolish mistake, yes, but one many of us activists make throughout America. There are so few of us who really spend time on the frontlines addressing needs like education, violence prevention, prison reentry programs, immigration and housing rights, and more, that we wind up working 18 to 20 hour days, ignoring our own personal finances and our health (I am in great health, but I have not had health insurance in several years), and we become that person everyone in the community calls upon for help, no matter what the issue or the cause. Add to that, which being a public speaker, which basically means being an independent contractor responsible for estimating your own taxes year to year, and that is how I wound up with back taxes.

It was not until early 2006, when a friend offered me the very rare opportunity to purchase his Downtown Brooklyn condo for no money down that I began to think about my finances in a very different kind of way. I had been living as a renter in the same basement apartment for eight years, but was being forced to move on due to my landlady's mother needing the space because of cancer and inability to climb stairs any longer. I did not want to rent again, so I jumped at this opportunity to be an owner. But I could not do it alone, so I asked my mother, still frugal all these years later with her own limited finances, to purchase the condo. She did, with the agreement that I would pay the monthly mortgages. We closed on the condo in June 2006, and I was immediately given a crash course in property ownership.

I naively believed that I could pay a monthly mortgage on two loans totaling approximately $5000 because I often made that in speaking fees. Wrong. Although the recession did not officially hit until 2008, we were feeling tremors of it as early as the Fall of 2006 when I was suddenly not getting the number of paid gigs I had been accustomed to.

So the past four years have been about making ends meet, just as my mother did when I was a child, just as many in Brooklyn and throughout America are doing in these times. And I've had to make some very tough decisions, the same kinds of tough decisions many in Brooklyn's 10th Congressional district have had to make: Pay the mortgage or pay the estimated taxes? It is tough for those of us without preferential or V.I.P. mortgages like the current Congressman representing my district.

And my accountant and I purposely estimated high on my campaign's recent financial disclosure statement, as we are still talking with the IRS about what the actual amount is. It is definitely not what is on the financial disclosure statement. This is a process, but one that is happening, because I am a man and a leader who takes responsibility for all my actions, always. And only with this second accountant, and a great attorney, over these past few years, have I been able to correct a lot of previous mistakes made, including bad contracts I unwittingly signed for various business deals that went south.

That said, I live a very basic life at this point, my mother and I are no longer in danger of losing this condo, my accountant and my lawyer have gotten all my financial obligations under control, and many are paid off or in the process of being paid off.

And after all these up and down financial tribulations, I feel very strongly they actually make me uniquely qualified to serve the people of Brooklyn's 10th Congressional districts. For their experiences are my experiences. There was no greater example of this than one night when I was campaigning in Boerum Hill, and myself and Jacob Bloomfield, one of our volunteers, stumbled upon a 50ish man with a slight limp. When we tried to give him campaign literature, he yelled and cursed and told us how useless politicians were as he struggled to hold onto his home for the sake of his wife and two daughters.

We put down our campaign literature, and sat down with that man for nearly an hour listening to his life story: how he became injured and disabled; how his bank is trying to take his home; how he called the current Congressman's office and got no help whatsoever. He was near tears at some points, and I felt his pain. When done, he thanked us for listening and, in spite of his own dire circumstances, offered a $100 donation to our campaign, and he has been a volunteer ever since.

And I encounter these kinds of stories all over Brooklyn's 10th Congressional district. Of people who are behind on their taxes, like me. Of people who have struggled, at times, to hold on to their homes, like me. Of people who have not always been financially literate, like me, but who, like me, have become so out of experience and necessity.

This is our America, these are our stories, and these are our truths, raw and unfiltered, sometimes pretty, sometimes not. And, again, if I did not really love and care about people, if I did not really believe that I, as a leader, could make a serious difference, in Brooklyn and in Washington, I would not put my entire life on display like this for others to poke and prod at will.

I do so because I feel this is what every single public servant should do. We serve the people, not the other way around, and the people have the right to know everything about us if we claim to be representing them.

Why Are We Killing Troy Davis?

SEPTEMBER 2011
PUBLISHED IN THE GUARDIAN

"To take a life when a life has been lost is revenge, not justice."
- *Desmond Tutu*

Unless something God-like and miraculous happens, Troy Davis, 42, is going to be executed tomorrow, Wednesday, September 21, 2011, at 7pm, by lethal injection at a state prison in Jackson, Georgia.

Let me say up front I feel great sorrow for the family of Mark MacPhail, the police officer who was shot and murdered on August 19, 1989. I cannot imagine the profound pain they've shouldered for 22 angst-filled years, hoping, waiting, and praying for some semblance of justice. Officer MacPhail will never come back to life, his wife, his two children, and his mother will never see him again. Under that sort of emotional and spiritual duress, I can imagine why they are convinced Troy Davis is the murderer of their beloved son, husband, and father.

But, likewise, I feel great sorrow for Troy Davis and his family. I don't know if Mr. Davis murdered Officer MacPhail or not. What I do know is that there is no DNA evidence linking him to the crime, that seven of nine witnesses have either recanted

KEVIN POWELL

or contradicted their original testimonies tying him to the act, and that a gentleman named Sylvester "Redd" Coles is widely believed to be the actual triggerman. But no real case against Mr. Coles has ever been pursued.

So a man is going to be executed, murdered, in fact, under a dark cloud of doubt in a nation, ours, that has come to practice executions as effortlessly as we breath.

Be it Republican presidential candidate Rick Perry, governor of Texas, and the 234 executions that have occurred under his watch (that fact was cheered loudly at a recent Republican debate), or the 152 executions when George W. Bush was governor of that state, we are a nation of an eye for an eye, a tooth for a tooth, a life for a life. Spiraling so far out of control that we are going to execute someone who may actually be innocent tomorrow.

I say we because the blood of Officer MacPhail and Troy Davis will be on the hands of us all. We Americans who fail to use our individual and collective voices to deal with the ugliness in our society that leads to violence in the first place, be they for economic crimes or because some of us have simply been driven mad by the pressures of trying to exist in a world that often marginalizes or rejects us. Thus our solution for many problems often becomes force, or violence. But it has long since been proven that the death penalty or capital punishment is not a deterrent, contrary to some folks' beliefs. Murders continue to happen every single day in America, as commonplace as apple pie, football, and Ford trucks.

I also say we because it is startling to me that Troy Davis could be on death row for twenty years, have his guilt be under tremendous doubt, yet save a few dedicated souls and organizations, there has not been a mass movement of support to save his life, to end the death penalty, not by well-meaning Black folks, not by well-meaning White folks, not by well-meaning folks of any stripe, and certainly not by influential Black folks who represent the corridors of power in places like Atlanta, with the exception of, say, Congressman John Lewis.

You wonder what the outcome of the parole board decision would have been if Black churches in Atlanta and other parts of Georgia, for example, had joined this cause to end the death penalty in America years back, if Black leaders had launched a sustained action much in the way their religious and spiritual foremothers and forefathers had done two generations before? What could have been different if more Georgia ministers had the courage of Atlanta's Rev. Dr. Raphael Gamaliel Warnock, pastor of the famed Ebenezer Baptist Church once helmed by Dr. King? Dr. Warnock has been steadfast and outspoken, yet seemingly out there alone in his support of Troy Davis. I mean if there is ever a time for Black churches to practice a relevant ministry, as Dr. King once urged, is it not when a seeming injustice like the Troy Davis matter is right in front of our faces? When so many Black males are locked up in America's prisons? What is the point, really, of having a "men's ministry" at your church if it is not addressing one of the major problems of the 21st century, that of the Black male behind bars? Especially in a society, America, that incarcerates more people than any other nation on earth.

And you wonder how the five-person Georgia State Board

of Pardons and Parole that, paradoxically, includes two Black males, including the head of the board, must feel. Had it not been for past legal injustices, like the Scottsboro Boys case of the 1930s or the vicious killing of Emmett Till in the 1950s, there would not have been a Civil Rights Movement, nor the placement of Blacks in places to balance the scales of justice, like that Georgia Parole Board. While I certainly do not think any Black person should get a pass just because they are Black, I do think, if you are an aware Black man, somewhere in your psyche has to be some residual memory of Black males being lynched in America, of Black male after Black male being sent to jail, or given the death penalty, under often flimsy charges and evidence. If there is a reasonable doubt, keep the case open until there is ultimate certainty—

Finally, incredibly ironic and tragic that this is happening while our first Black president is sitting in the White House. We, America, like to pat ourselves on the back and say job well done whenever there is a shred of racial or social progress in our fair nation. But then we habitually figure out ways to take one, two, several steps back, with this Troy Davis execution, with the rise of the Tea Party and its thinly-veiled racial paranoia politics, to push America right back to the good old says of segregation, Jim Crow, brute hatred of those who are different, while social inequalities run rampant like rats in the night.

And if you think Troy Davis' cause celebre has nothing to do with Jim Crow, then either you've not been to an American prison lately, or you simply are blind. I've been to many, across our country, and they are filled to the brim with mostly Black and Latino males (and some poor White males), including the majority of folks sitting on death row.

For sure, given my background of poverty, a single mother, an absent father, and violence and great economic despair in my childhood and teen years, but for the grace of God I could be one of those young Black or Latino males languishing in jail at this very moment. I could be, indeed, Troy Davis.

So I cannot simply view the Troy Davis case and execution as solely about the killing of Officer MacPhail. Yes, an injustice was done, a killing occurred, and I pray the truth really comes out one day.

But I am just as concerned about America's soul, of the morality tales we are text-messaging to ourselves, to the world, as we move Troy Davis from his cell one last time, to that room where a needle will blast death into his veins, suck the air from his throat, snatch life from his eyes.

While the family of Mr. Davis and the family of Officer MacPhail converge, one final time, to witness a death in progress—

Now two men will be dead, Officer MacPhail and Troy Davis, linked, forever, by the misfortune of our confusion, stereotypes, finger-pointing, and history of passing judgment without having every shred of the facts. I am Officer MacPhail, I am Troy Davis, and so are you. And you. And you, too.

And as my mother would say, have mercy on us all, Lawd, for we know not what we do—

Black Leadership Is Dead

OCTOBER 2010
PUBLISHED IN EBONY

Black leadership is dead. There, I said it. We have people in leadership positions, but far too many of them are operating as if it were the 1960s or even the 1980s instead of the twenty-first century.

As I've traveled from state to state over the years, I've heard folks saying that "we need another Malcolm, we need another Martin," as if dynamic hip-hop generational leaders like Malia Lazu, Ras Baraka, April Silver, Shani Jamila, and Brian Echols don't even exist. In fact, I can easily count off 100 such leaders from coast to coast—all of who are doing incredible work in their communities.

We seem to have forgotten the old axiom that all movements are local. Black America has been pining for a national savior since the Civil Rights Movement came to a screeching halt in the 1970s. Apart from our flirtations with Rev. Jesse Jackson and Min. Louis Farrakhan in the 1980s and 90s, we've been stuck in the wilderness without any sort of national Black leadership model for forty long and difficult years.

Want to know why large pockets of Black America remain in great despair despite all our amazing post-Civil Rights era advances? Well, look no further than the incredible lack of vision and imagination of our Black leaders—be they elected officials, ministers and imams, public intellectuals, heads of social service organizations, educators, entrepreneurs, or grassroots activists.

Black American leadership has been in a state of arrested development since the days of Fannie Lou Hamer, Ella Baker, the Student Nonviolent Coordinating Committee, Angela Davis, and the Black Panther Party. But some leaders were killed or driven mad by those times, while others wound up in jail or sold out their principles for access to the American dream, for themselves and their immediate circle, rather than for us all. Little wonder, then, that so many of us have pinned our dreams on Barack Obama in 2008. Someone like him was a long time a-coming.

But, no, President Barack Obama is not a Black leader; he is the President of the United States of America. Not the President of Black America, or of hip-hop America, or of young America. Just America. And therein lies the great irony of Mr. Obama being the first Black president in American history. There is this great expectation that President Obama will be that liberator for us, the modern-day Malcolm X-meets-Dr. King, with a swagger that fuses the jazz of John Coltrane and the hip hop of Jay-Z.

But some in Black America have been hard on President Obama for not being, well, Black enough for their taste. Part of the reason for this feeling is the huge void in visionary Black leadership. We've been stuck in this vacuum for so long that we expect Mr. Obama to fill it up for us. We expect him to tell it like it is on race and racism, and fulfill all the needs of Black America.

That is not only completely unfair to Mr. Obama, but it speaks of the desperation surrounding our lack of leadership. Many of us are still searching for the sort of leader that has never existed in the White House, or in the statehouse, or in any city's City Hall.

Meanwhile, we ourselves are scattered, unfocused, and constantly reacting instead of being proactive. We react to the police murders of Sean Bell (New York) and Oscar Grant (the Bay Area), to the Tea Party, Glenn Beck, and Rush Limbaugh, and to gentrification, mass unemployment and mass incarceration, but where are our proactive local and national agendas?

Yes, no doubt racism is alive and well in America. In spite of all its proclamations to the contrary, America has never had the kind of national conversation about race we truly need. This is not a matter of somebody just giving a speech, no matter how eloquent. What we require is something akin to the truth and reconciliation commission established in South Africa after the fall of apartheid.

But what armchair critics of Barack Obama fail to grasp, in historical terms, is that it has always been the people, not the person in the White House, who pushed our nation forward. If there were no abolitionist movement led by the likes of Frederick Douglass, then there would have been no Emancipation Proclamation by President Lincoln. Without A.

Phillip Randolph and others threatening a massive protest in Washington, then Franklin Roosevelt would not have banned discrimination within World War II industries. And with no Civil Rights Movement, there would be no Civil Rights Bill in 1964 and no Voting Rights Act in 1965.

Whoever has occupied the White House has always had to face harsh critics. And W.E.B. DuBois, an intellectual giant who lived well into his 90s, was chief among them. But current sideline critics and some of these multimedia hustlers posing as intellectuals ought to study DuBois a bit more closely. Not only was he a scholar, a prolific writer, and a true renaissance man interacting with Black people globally, but he also helped to build institutions that served the people, including the N.A.A.C.P. He didn't just dog out a sitting president and leave it there.

DuBois understood that talk can be wonderful, but nothing beats action. And that's the principle behind the N.A.A.C.P. before that organization went adrift. A strong difference of opinion on the best way to deal with racism is what led DuBois out of the N.A.A.C.P. in the mid-1930s. Here's a small part of his stinging critique:

"Today this organization, which has been great and effective for nearly a quarter of a century, finds itself in a time of crisis and change, without a program, without effective organization, without executive officers who have either the ability or disposition to guide [it] in the right direction."

Sound familiar?

DuBois was addressing the need for Black institutions of all kinds. Something that is still badly needed in Black America in 2010.

No wonder we are at such a crossroads in Black American history. On the one hand we have groups like the N.A.A.C.P., which seem so spooked by right-wing zealots that they allow a Shirley Sherrod to go down without making sure the people hear the truth, or even listen to her entire speech. On the other end of the spectrum are all the Barack-haters, folks who never seem to miss an opportunity to verbally assault the President every chance they get. That would include certain motor-mouth Black Ph.D.s, and the sort of media pundits who have much to say about the Black community, but who are rarely ever seen in any Black community except when it's time for a drive-by photo opportunity.

All this noise makes for great headlines and television ratings, but does absolutely nothing to empower Black America.

It really is a sad joke. Doubly sad when you consider the many challenges we face, including the HIV/AIDS pandemic, nonstop violence in all forms, serious health problems like diabetes, high blood pressure, and obesity, and the lack of respect afforded to both our elders and our youth.

Black leadership will continue to be dead if we waste our time heaving hate at Barack Obama, or waiting for him to solve all our problems. We ourselves must rise to meet the challenge. The question is what are you doing, in your local community, on a consistent basis, to build or support institutions that help our people to help themselves?

My job as a leader, and your job, too—if you care enough—is to support true visionary leaders. Folks like Charlie Braxton in Jackson, Mississippi—a handicapped Black man who works day to day, thanklessly and often anonymously, with and for the people. I have seen Charlie bring feuding gang members together, mentor all kinds of young people, create one business after another, and serve as a beacon of light for a community where so many other lights are dimmed.

That is the new model of Black leadership in the twenty-first century: build or maintain institutions that provide direct service, resources, and information to our communities; change, once and for all, how we discuss the many challenges facing our people; and be on the front lines with the people as much as possible.

When we can do that—and identify and support more who do—then we in Black America will have a real shot of getting out of this wilderness. But if we do not, then it will be another long 40 years looking for a Moses who may never come.

Charlie Rangel Begat Ed Towns: Something Is Broken In Brooklyn, Too

JULY 2010
PUBLISHED IN HUFFINGTON POST

"Nearly all men can stand adversity, but if you want to test a man's character, give him power."
- *Abraham Lincoln*

And the drama of Congressman Charlie Rangel continues to unfold with 13 charges of misconduct, even as I type this essay: Mr. Rangel faces a range of accusations stemming from his accepting four rent-stabilized apartments, to misusing his office to preserve a tax loophole worth half a billion dollars for an oil executive who pledged a donation for an educational center being built in Mr. Rangel's honor. In short, Mr. Rangel, one of the most powerful Democrats in the United States House of Representatives, has given his Republican foes much fodder to attack Dems as the November mid-term elections quickly approach.

While this saga continues, two questions dangle in the air:

First, where did it all go so terribly wrong? And, second, did Mr. Rangel begat the lack of ethics also present in the career of his colleague, friend, and staunch ally Congressman Edolphus "Ed" Towns of Brooklyn, New York?

http://beta.wnyc.org/blogs/azi-paybarah/2010/jul/28/towns-rangel-going-be-there/

To answer these questions I think we must go back to the 1960s and the Civil Rights Movement's waning days. Dr. King was still alive, but his popularity had plummeted, which explains why, to this day, many people do not know his writings or sermons from those latter years. Congressman Adam Clayton Powell, Jr. of Harlem (Mr. Rangel's predecessor) was clinging to his seat amidst ethics battles of his own. The streets of Black America were habitually afire, as urban unrest became the language of the unheard ghetto masses. And in majority Black communities like Harlem and Brooklyn, Black leaders, emboldened by Civil Rights victories, chants of "Black Power," and a once-in-a-century opportunity for power, rushed through the kicked-in doors, into politics, into business, into film and television, into book publishing and magazines (or started their own), and into colleges and universities heretofore shuttered. It was the best of times and it was the worst of times. The best because many really believed "change" was on the horizon. The worst because some Black movers and shakers were so happy to get inside that they came with no vision or a plan whatsoever for their followers.

Clearly very few even bothered to read Dr. King's landmark essay "Black Power Redefined," which sought to push Black leaders toward a programmatic agenda that included the poor and economically disenfranchised.

And if there were any communities in Black America to test Dr. King's vision, they were Harlem and Brooklyn. Brooklyn has Black America's largest concentration of people of African descent. But Harlem, in particular, was the symbolic capital of Black America, and it was there that the now famous Gang of Four—Percy Sutton, Charlie Rangel, David Dinkins, and Basil Paterson—planned and plotted a course for their community, and themselves. Rangel replaced Powell in Congress and became the dean of New York politics. Sutton would first be a successful politician himself, then eventually start Inner City Broadcasting, a major person of color owned media enterprise; Basil Paterson would be, among other things, New York State Senator, Deputy Mayor of New York City, and New York Secretary of State; and David Dinkins, of course, became the first Black mayor of New York City.

Truth be told Mr. Rangel and his colleagues had an incredible vision and really did nothing differently than their White predecessors had been doing for decades in America: they saw an opportunity for a taste of power and they took it. (And at least the Gang of Four brought an economic empowerment zone to Harlem, something Congressman Towns pretended to want to do in the mid1990s for Brooklyn, then mysteriously backed away from, instead endorsing then-Mayor Rudolph Giuliani's re-election bid, with Brooklyn never hearing about that zone again.)

Indeed, as I was coming of age as a student and youth activist in the 1980s, and as a then-reporter with various Black newspapers in the New York City area, I remember well hearing their names mentioned often. And, to a lesser extent, the names of their Black political peers in Brooklyn like Al Vann, Major Owens, and Sonny Carson. It was awe-inspiring, because I did not know that Black folks were leaders in this way. The pinnacle of this Black political ascension in New York City, without question, was the election of David Dinkins in 1989. For New York was the last of the major American cities to produce a Black mayor.

But something stopped during Dinkins' years in City Hall. Black New York was unable to shake off the catastrophic effects of the 1980s crack cocaine scourge, or Reagan-era social policies. Meanwhile, Black leadership in New York, rather than nurture and prepare the next generation of Black voices to succeed them, did exactly what their White forerunners had done: they dug their heels deeper into the sands of power and have instead become leaders of what I call "a ghetto monarchy." In other words, the community-first values of the Civil Rights era have been replaced by the post-Civil Rights era values of me-first, career first, and control and domination of my building, my block, my housing projects, my district, my part of the community (if not all of it), my church, my community center, or my organization, by any means necessary. For as long as possible. And often for as much money, privilege, and access to power as one can get with a "career" as a Black leader or figurehead.

And that, my friends, is what leads us, again, to the sad spectacles of the two senior most Congresspersons in New York State: Charlie Rangel of Harlem, and my representative in Brooklyn, Congressman Edolphus "Ed" Towns.

For it is so clear that the leadership path of Congressman Rangel begat the leadership path of Congressman Towns. Both may have been well intentioned at the beginning of their careers. Both may very well believe in the goodness, as I do, of public service for the people. But something has gone terribly wrong, the longer they have stayed in office (40 years now, for Mr. Rangel, and 27 long years for Mr. Towns); something that, I believe, has zapped them of their ability to serve effectively. That has zapped them of sound moral, political and ethical judgment. That has led both to be disconnected from the very people they claim to serve, both younger and older people alike.

And you see this pattern with old school Black political leaders nationwide. For ghettoes exist wherever you see Black city council or alderpersons. Ghettoes exist wherever you see Black state senators and assemblypersons. And ghettoes exist for most of the Congressional districts, too, represented by Black House members. 40-plus long years of Black political representation, in record numbers, in fact, but it seems our communities are worse off than even before the Civil Rights Movement.

Now I am very clear that systemic racism has done a number on these communities from coast to coast, from how financial institutions have treated urban areas, to the deterioration of our public schools when White flight became real in the 1960s and 1970s, to loss of factories, and other job incubators, to the often combative relationship between our communities and local police. And let us not begin to talk about the effects of gentrification on urban areas across America the past decade and a half.

But if a leader really has any vision, she or he figures out some way to help the people to help themselves. You simply do not retreat to what is safe, secure, and predictable in terms of your actions, or lack thereof. Doing that means you simply have given up. Or, worse, you just do not care.

For me, no clearer evidence than the other day when I was campaigning for Congress in Marcy Projects in the Bedford-Stuyvesant section of Brooklyn, the Marcy Projects made famous in the lyrics of hiphop superstar and Brooklyn native son Jay-Z. 60-year-old Marcy Projects is so huge a housing complex that it swallows whole Myrtle and Park and Flushing Avenues between Nostrand and Marcy. It consists of 27 buildings, over 1700 apartments, and approximately 5000 residents. And except for areas like Fort Greene (excluding its own projects), Clinton Hill, Boerum Hill, and parts of Dumbo, Bed-Stuy, East Flatbush, and Canarsie, most of Mr. Towns' district is as impoverished, under-served, and as forgotten as Marcy Projects.

There is the sight of several elderly women sitting on benches in the middle of this aging complex, frustrated with the state of their lives, their meager incomes, the bags of garbage strewn about them, and the rats who have created dirt holes so big around each building, that a small human head could fit through most of those holes. When I ask these women where is the nearest senior citizen center so they could have some measure of relief, they say, in unison, "Right here, outside, where we are sitting now, these benches. This is the safest place we got."

There is the sight of children, pre-teens and teens, running, jumping, over pissed stained asphalt, scraping their knees on the ground filled with broken bottles and broken promises. There also is no community center open in Marcy any longer. Why that is the case, no Marcy resident can tell me. What they do tell me is that Marcy Playground is being renovated. And indeed it is. But the residents feel it is not for them, that it is for "the new White people coming into the area, and the new Black people who have some money."

There is the sight of all those Black and Latino males standing on this or that corner, in front of this or that building, the hands of their lives shoved deep into their pockets, their hunger for something better fed by a Newport cigarette, a taste of malt liquor or Hennessey, a pull on a marijuana stick. And then the ritual happens: a police car shows up, males and females of all ages are asked for identification, are thrown up against a wall, against the squad car, or to the ground, asked where they live, where they are going, why are they standing there, what is in their shoes, in their underwear. Or they are accused of trespassing for going from one building to another, even if they are simply visiting a relative or friend.

This is not just life in Marcy Projects, Bed-Stuy, Brooklyn. This is what ghetto monarchs like Congressman Towns and

Congressman Rangel preside over in Black communities nationwide. Perhaps, once more, they really cared at one point— maybe they really did. But circa 2010, Charlie Rangel's problems are Ed Towns' problems because the apple does not fall very far from the tree. Yes, cite Mr. Rangel's litany of indiscretions, but let us not forget Mr. Towns' own timeline of indiscretions while overseeing his district (see the timeline below for Mr. Towns), for nearly three decades, with, among other things, some of the bloodiest violence in America, the highest HIV/AIDS rates in America, the most under-achieving schools (with a few notable exceptions), and vast disparities between the haves and the have-nots. Right here in Brooklyn, New York.

Is it little wonder that as I travel this Congressional district, meeting with Jewish folks in Boerum HIill, Chinese folks in Williamsburg, West Indian folks in East Flatbush and Canarsie, or African American and Puerto Rican folks in East New York, I hear the same things time and again: "We never see Mr. Towns except maybe when he needs our vote" or "I have never seen Mr. Towns in my life" or "I have called Mr. Towns' office many times and never gotten the help I need" or "I just do not trust any of these politicians at all. They all lie."

This is why voter turnout is perpetually low. This is why incumbents get to stay in office decade after decade. The formula is very simple for electeds like Congressman Ed Towns: Identify the loyal voters and only cater to them (helping them get election poll jobs, or regular jobs, helping their children get into schools, paying for trips out of town to some casino or amusement park or cookout). Stay out of sight of all the other registered

Democratic voters, banking on them simply pulling the lever for "Democrats" every election cycle without any fuss or questions. Never debate an insurgent opponent for fear of your being exposed for who you really are, and for what you have not done for the community. Turn your political seat into a business, one where your family member and circle of friends and colleagues benefit from the powerful reach of your position.

So why would you want to give that up? Why would you even bother to do more than is absolutely necessary when you are able to enjoy the perks of a long political career without much effort, without much sweat equity at all? Why would you even think that taking on the values of political corruption are unethical at all, if there has been no one to hold you accountable for so very long?

And why would you see that Brooklyn, and the Brooklyns of America, are broken, so very terribly broken, even though it is clear as day to the people in your community?

The Mess at
Medgar Evers College

JANUARY 2011
PUBLISHED IN DAILY KOS

"You can kill a man but you can't kill an idea."—MEDGAR EVERS
(NAACP Field Secretary in Mississippi murdered by Ku Klux
Klan in 1963)

And, no doubt, Medgar Evers must be tossing and turning
in his grave at Arlington National Cemetery this very moment.
For how terrible is it that a college named in his honor is in the
midst of the ugliest chapter of its long history, a history born of
the sweat, and the blood, of the Civil Rights Movement?

The problem, to put it mildly, are the president and the
provost of Medgar Evers College, two Black men who, by virtue of
one baffling action after another, demonstrate no respect for the
mission of a school built in the heart of Black Brooklyn, and who
ostensibly have little to no respect for faculty and staff, nor the
community that surrounds that institution. That their behavior
and mindset are akin to the Southern White segregationists of
the Civil Rights era who went out of their way to block, literally

KEVIN POWELL

and symbolically, the doors of their schools rather than allow Black students in, must be something the president and provost have conveniently forgotten. That the leadership of the City University of New York, which governs all 23 of the four- and two-year schools in its system, has allowed this now very public spectacle to fester and rot begs this question: Who really cares about the mission and future of Medgar Evers College?

I mean, seriously, would this blog and the protests and pending lawsuits be necessary if we were discussing, say, John Jay College, Lehman College, or Medgar's borough cousin, Brooklyn College?

No—

However, we are talking about Medgar Evers College, though not technically an historically Black college in fact, but certainly so in its creation, sense of purpose, and the overwhelming numbers in terms of faculty, staff, and students. Indeed, for those who do not know, Medgar Evers College is a four-year commuter school of 7000 students nestled in what we call Central Brooklyn. Brooklyn is not only the largest of New York City's five boroughs (with 2.5-3 million residents we would be America's 4th most populated "city"), but Brooklyn also contains the biggest Black population in our nation (nearly 1 million people of African descent from across America, and the globe).

And the original mission of Medgar Evers College, as stated currently on its website at http://www.mec.cuny.edu/presidents_office/mec_mission.asp, was "a result of collaborative efforts by community leaders, elected officials, the Chancellor, and the Board of Trustees of The City University of New York. The College, named for the late civil rights leader, Medgar Wiley Evers (1925-1963), was established in 1969 and named in 1970, with a mandate to meet the educational and social needs of the Central Brooklyn community. The College is committed to the fulfillment of this mandate."

Obviously someone didn't mention this bit of history and purpose to President William Pollard or Provost Howard Johnson. Or perhaps the duo has simply not bothered to read the website during their tenure. Because in my 20 years of living in Brooklyn, and an extensive association with that school—as a community and political leader; as a writer and artist; as someone who has given numerous lectures there, and participated in more panels, conferences, and seminars than I can count, there; and as an ally and supporter with my own critiques of Medgar Evers College—never could I have imagined, when these two took over the leadership in August of 2009, such a swift and abrupt deterioration of the way the school is administered.

Immediate past president Dr. Edison O. Jackson definitely was no perfect leader, either, but you at least got the sense he genuinely loved the school and the community about the school. Conversely, at a chance encounter with President Pollard the summer of 2010, I came away thinking the man not only did not like Brooklyn (it took everything in me not to suggest he should leave if he despised it, and us Brooklynites, so much), but that Mr. Pollard was eager to do whatever he could to dismantle the inner mechanisms of Medgar Evers College, even the parts that were working just fine. It is one thing, as a leader, to put your own stamp on an enterprise you are now running, as every leader should have her or his vision on how things should be. It is quite another to give the appearance of destroying that enterprise entirely, with reckless abandon, just because you can—

Yet I am not even sure if "incompetent" is the right word to describe what is happening here. But it is abundantly clear to me, when one reviews the backgrounds of President Pollard and Provost Johnson prior to their coming to Medgar Evers College, that whoever thought these two gentlemen deserved to run a major institution for higher learning must not have seen any of the numerous articles critical of their prior escapades.

In Mr. Pollard's case, we are talking allegations of the gross mismanagement of millions of dollars at his previous job as president of the University of the District of Columbia:

http://image2.examiner.com/a-1072664~UDC_chief_details_waste_of_millions.html

In Mr. Johnson's case, we are talking allegations of the plagiarizing of an academic plan from Syracuse University, where he formerly worked, and which he gave to his new employer, the University of North Texas:

http://www.dailyorange.com/2.8654/plagiarism-by-administrator-unacceptable-1.1241774

So is it little wonder that since the arrival of Mr. Pollard and Mr. Johnson in August 2009 we have the present mess at Medgar Evers College, including:

1) Some very curious faculty dismissals

2) Threats of shutting down academic centers on the campus

3) Faculty concerns about the administration's lack of respect for shared governance (in the past month 66 faculty members (89% of those who voted), mostly tenured, cast a vote of "no confidence" in the president and the provost)

4) No strategic plan by the president or the provost, after one year on their jobs, on the future of Medgar Evers College

5) The Provost eliminated the Writing Center and the Center for Teaching and Learning (what college does not have a Writing Center?)

6) The Administration removed Carver Bank ATMs (Carver is the largest Black-owned bank in America) and replaced them with Citibank ATMs

7) The Administration issued an eviction notice for The Center for NuLeadership; and although the proposal for formal approval of the Center under CUNY guidelines was approved before the current administration came into power, the President

and Provost have refused to forward the proposal to CUNY

For a full accounting of faculty, staff, and community concerns, please check this excellent blog: *http://eisaulen.com/blog///index. php/2011/01/02/interview-is-medgar-evers-college-under-attack- faculty-battle-provost-and-president*

And there are many more issues, but the one that sticks out to me is the apparent attack by the Medgar Evers College administration on the Center for NuLeadership on Urban Solutions. As was stated in a recent press release, the Center for NuLeadership "is the first and only public policy, research, training, advocacy and academic center housed in the largest urban university system in the United States, conceived, designed, and developed by formerly incarcerated professionals."

In other words, these are not just "ex-cons" running wild at Medgar Evers College. These are individuals like Dr. Divine Pryor, formerly incarcerated person, who has turned his life around and become a valuable asset to community and academia. And I can honestly say, in my travels throughout America, to literally hundreds upon hundreds of colleges and universities, community centers and religious institutions, and jails and prisons of every kind, that I have never encountered someone who is as articulate, dynamic, and passionate in identifying ways to stop the school-to-prison pipeline so real for American ghettos as Dr. Pryor.

And if Medgar Evers College was founded with the expressed purpose of meeting "the educational and social needs of the

Central Brooklyn community," then does it not make sense to house a center that deals directly with the record numbers of Black (and Latino) males being shipped off to jail each and every year, in Brooklyn, and all the Brooklyns in America?

Not by the logic of President Pollard and Provost Johnson. Perhaps that is why these two Black males, along with CUNY central administration officials, saw nothing wrong with a December 17, 2010 late-night "raid" of NuLeadership's offices, and the seizure of computers personally owned by Dr. Pryor and his colleague Kate Kyung Ji Rhee.

Or why the Center for NuLeadership was asked to vacate its offices by December 30th (the center had to go to court to block the eviction, temporarily).

Or why the president and the provost have refused to forward the recommendation by the college's governing body to establish, officially, the center at Medgar Evers College.

Or why the president and the provost have blocked the Center for NuLeadership's funds, and refused to approve a $2.4 million grant that would have given first-time non-violent offenders a second chance by sentencing them to college rather than prison.

The great sadness and irony of these two Black male administrators doing this at a college born to better the most underserved parts of Brooklyn is not lost on me. Doubly sad and ironic that we have a President of the United States (Barack Obama) and a Secretary of Education (Arne Duncan) who have consistently called for innovative solutions to prepare and propel the most marginalized populations in America.

And sad and ironic, furthermore, because the City University of New York actually has a system-wide Black male initiative. But how can we seriously discuss any initiatives for Black males and not include in that conversation ideas and best practices to cease the rapid flow of Black (and Latino) men in and out of the criminal justice system?

So as we approach the annual Dr. King holiday in less than two weeks, the president and provost of Medgar Evers College and the City University of New York hierarchy find themselves with a major dilemma, bad publicity, and unnecessary and very preventable beefs, in and out of court, with Medgar Evers faculty and staff, and Brooklyn community members. As one tenured professor at Medgar Evers College said to me in an email, what is happening at the school "should be a national outrage."

For sure, the mess at Medgar Evers College is a national outrage, and a deeply moral failing, too, especially at a time in our history when America's inner cities require, need, demand, nonstop and pro-active solutions and remedies, and as many opportunities as possible for our communities, particularly for the young and the poor.

And wasn't that the point of Medgar Evers College in the first place, to serve the people?

Troy Davis Is Not Dead

SEPTEMBER 2011
PUBLISHED IN HUFFINGTON POST

T here is yet another great and bloody gash on the soul of America right now, because we allowed a state-sponsored killing of a potentially innocent man to occur in our name, on our watch. Fellow Americans, we must end the uncivilized and inhuman act of the death penalty, of killing people convicted of or believed to be murderers, immediately. If slavery was barbaric and morally wrong in its time, then the death penalty is barbaric and morally wrong in ours. Troy Davis should not be physically dead but, alas, he is.

I feel immense sorrow, was unable to sleep last night, and my very sincere prayers are both with the family of slain police officer Mark MacPhail, and with Troy Davis' loved ones. We have two tragic life endings on our hands, separated by 22 years, millions of dollars in taxpayer money, and bottomless divisions in how and why a murder case should be handled and judged. For in executing Troy Davis he has been made a martyr, a symbol of a new movement of awareness about our very busted criminal justice system, of how much race and class come into play when deciding who will be imprisoned, and for how long, who will be executed, and why, and what people are more likely to be executed for killing those not their race. Specifically when Black folks are charged with killing White folks. And, yes, I am aware that a White man named Lawrence Russell Brewer of Texas was executed, coincidentally, on the same day as Troy Davis, for the 1998 truck-dragging murder of a Black man, James Byrd. But, one, it is so rare that a White person is ever convicted (or put to death) for the killing of a Black person, or a Latino person, or an Asian person or a Native American person, in our America. And, second and most important, I am in complete opposition to the death penalty, and that means I did not want Mr. Brewer to be executed either, no matter how apparent his guilt was in the James Byrd death. Neither Lawrence Russell Brewer nor Troy Davis should be physically dead but, alas, they are.

Yet in spite of the racial realities of America, still, a progressive, multicultural army of concerned citizens came together to make our voices heard, in support of Troy Davis, in opposition to the death penalty. I have been an activist of some sort for 27 long years and I can tell you of the numerous movements and mini-movements I've ever been a part of, few have been as empowering and uplifting as the work to spare Troy Davis' life. You could see and feel this online, on Facebook, on Twitter, in the many email exchanges and forwards. You could see and feel this in the too-many-to-count blogs that have been posted. And I certainly could feel and see it last night at our Brooklyn, New York rally and vigil for Troy Davis, where people of all races, all faiths (or none at all), all avenues of life, came together, in solidarity, for a cause that mattered as much to them as their own lives.

That is why I think it important that well-meaning Americans of whatever background read Michelle Alexander's astonishing book *The New Jim Crow: Mass Incarceration in the Age of Colorblindness*. Ms. Alexander is a legal scholar and college professor who painstakingly puts down the facts about America's "prison-industrial complex," and how it has disproportionately affected people of color. I visit American prisons regularly and have seen first-hand the legions of Black and Latino males locked up for years, for life, or those languishing on death rows, awaiting their capital punishment. Troy Davis happens to be the most famous death penalty case in American history, but real change will only occur when we begin to understand this is a catastrophic crisis deeply woven into the American social fabric and justice system.

Yes, there should be penalties for crimes in America, but there is something critically wrong when Black males only make up a small percentage of the total American population yet are the highest percentile of American prison inmates, of inmates on death row, or individuals with criminal records which will follow many of them for the remainder of their physical lives. Indeed I thought of this and so much more as I assembled with that mostly young and very multicultural group at Downtown Brooklyn's The House of the Lord church for the Troy Davis rally and vigil last night. We had no real structure for the program, no idea what was going to happen, but we were clear, as were thousands of others similarly gathered across America, and the world, that we could not go through this modern-day lynching of Troy Davis alone. So we created spaces for ourselves, we burned candles, we marched, we rallied, we prayed, we cried, we held hands, and we Americans hugged strangers in a way I had not seen since the night Barack Obama was elected president and, before that, not since the September 11th tragedy.

For me personally my emotions and spirit felt twisted in a hurricane, like a thick tree broken at its root, because I could not help thinking that I, a Black male in America, could very easily be in Troy Davis' position. To be sure, some one hundred years ago, White males summarily murdered my great-grandfather, Baine Powell, from my mother's side of our Low Country South Carolina family, in his community because they coveted his business independence and his 400 acres of land. His widow was left with three mere acres and children to raise solo. As the story goes the fear and trauma left by the killing of my great-grandfather led many of my kinfolk to flee that community, fearing it could happen to them, too. While others stayed, paralyzed with that fear, the story passed from one generation to another in hushed tones of trepidation and warning.

Thus, for some Americans, there is a painful memory of lynchings, of people watching, celebrating, and smiling when a Black man was executed, in many cases for a crime with untrustworthy witnesses and flimsy evidence, as was the situation with Troy Davis. That is why so many took to the social networks and used the term lynching without apology.

And these were not just Black folks saying this either. For all Americans know, even in the quiet spaces of our minds, what America's shaky history is around justice. Matter of fact, when Larry Cox of Amnesty International came out of the Georgia Diagnostic and Classification Prison (yes, that is the real name) after witnessing Troy Davis' execution last night, he declared, pointedly, "I'm deeply ashamed of my country."

Does not mean that Mr. Cox, or any of us, are unpatriotic. On the contrary patriotism means, for me, that I love America so much, know its history so well, know its soul, heart, and mind so intimately, that I am clear what the potential is for America. But we will never achieve that potential, and will forever be semi-participants in the democracy and freedom social experiment, for ourselves, for the world, as long as things like the death penalty, poverty, ghettos, a dysfunctional public school system, and the absence of real-life economic opportunities for each and every American are alive and well.

So if there is ever a time for a national gut check, it is right here. For example, that means that so many people, especially in the state of Georgia, could have said their political careers are less important than murdering a potentially innocent man. Be it the five people who sit on the Georgia State Board of Pardons and Paroles, or the Chatham County (Savannah) District Attorney, or the judge who signed Troy Davis' death warrant on September 6, one after another refused to budge, or said they were powerless to do anything further. It makes you wonder how any of these folks can look themselves in the mirror on any given day, how they can, from one January to the next, celebrate the life and teachings of Georgia native son Martin Luther King, Jr., yet casually ignore one of his last lessons about us human beings needing to practice "a dangerous kind of selflessness." What these officials did, instead, was turn their ears and hearts off from people the world over, hid behind timid statements and telephone and fax busy signals, and either claimed someone else had more power than they, or they simply refused to acknowledge the 7 of 9 witnesses who recanted their stories, the lack of consistent and concrete evidence, and the moral outrage that poured in from Pope Benedict XVI, former president Jimmy Carter, former FBI Director (under President Ronald Reagan) William S. Sessions, Nobel Peace Prize winner Desmond Tutu, six prison wardens, and over one million signed petitions.

We can run but we cannot hide, and I sincerely hope the Troy Davis case also increases voter participation in Georgia threefold, especially among younger voters, and that Georgians vote out of office district attorneys, judges, and any elected official who did not listen to the cries of the people at an hour such as this. If not now, then when? If not for we the people, then for whom do you work? But this is what happens when people with clear and multiple political aspirations and clear and multiple political agendas put their careers and maneuverings for power ahead of the people. All the Georgia officials who, at one point or another over the past 20 years have crossed paths with the Troy Davis case, now have to live, for the rest of their physical lives, with the reality that they all took part in a state-sponsored murder. And did little to nothing to halt it.

Indeed, no one that I know, including me, was even remotely suggesting that Troy Davis should have been freed from jail. No. Just make it a life sentence is what I have stated publicly, especially under that huge cloud of doubt. But there is simply no way to kill the spirit of a man, a human being, who maintained his innocence right to the very end, as that lethal injection ended his life at 11:08Pm on Wednesday, September 21, 2011. As I said in a previous blog, I do not know what happened on the night of August 19, 1989, but I just cannot subscribe to the notion of an eye for an eye. If it was wrong for Officer MacPhail to be killed, then it was also wrong for Troy Davis to be killed. Either we human beings, in America, in the world, are going to practice peace, love, nonviolence, compassion, and mercy toward each other, or we are going to continue down a path toward the destruction of us all, one community after another, one nation after another, one life after another. I am not sure what God you worship, but the one I celebrate does not condone any of this. Likewise I categorically refuse to walk down that path of despair and hopelessness, for the work for justice is just beginning. Let us see the possibilities created by the short lives of both Officer Mark MacPhail and Troy Davis. Let us pray that the families of Officer MacPhail and Troy Davis one day come together to find the entire truth of what occurred, and become an extraordinary symbol of human unity and human understanding. Let us latch ourselves to that old but reliable mule called history and recall that it took a progressive, multicultural coalition of people power, committed for years, to end slavery in America. That same super-charged energy brought us the presidency of Barack

Obama in 2008. So I am convinced that we can come together, stay together, and be together, in this moment, to create a movement to end the death penalty in America and on this planet, once and for all.

And when we do this, Troy Davis' execution shall not be in vain—

An Open Letter to Black Male Athletes

OCTOBER 2011
PUBLISHED IN EBONY

My brothers:

I've wanted to write this open letter to all of you for a long time. That is because I am not only a huge admirer of what you do as sportsmen but also because I care, and I am deeply concerned about the state of Black male athletes in America today. You see, like many of you, I grew up with a single mother and an absent father in an impoverished ghetto environment with sports as one of the few outlets for my hopes and dreams, and my anger and frustrations, too. I played baseball, Little League through high school, and I also ran track all four years. On top of that, my interest in writing and reading had begun as a preteen and the very first books I absorbed were exciting histories of figures from baseball, football and basketball. So you could say that sports is in my blood, so much so that even when I worked at Vibe magazine years ago, I made it a point to step away from my writings on Tupac Shakur and other hip-hop stars to pen stories on ballplayers such as Chris Webber, Penny Hardaway and the

KEVIN POWELL

Dream Team II. And I certainly have a number of friends who are professional athletes today, as I have advised quite a few on matters from current decisions to future possibilities once their careers are over.

So I come to you not simply as a fan, but also as someone who knows well the inner workings of sports and entertainment; as someone who has seen far too many famous Black males, including 'Pac, get into trouble time and again with the law; and as someone who wants to see you live up to your full potential, not just as elite athletes, but as men.

That means I need to be blunt: There is a serious problem with the modern Black male athlete, which has become a sad and tragic scene, week to week, month after month, as one of you gets into trouble for infractions ranging from sexual assault and domestic violence accusations to allegations of drunk driving or drunken tirades at parties or strip clubs.

I am very clear that many of you were never given a blueprint for life, nor healthy, proactive definitions of manhood, nor practical advice on how to handle fame and millions of dollars so young and so suddenly. I am also very clear that not all Black male athletes get into trouble, that many of you are doing great work in your communities, adhering to your religious tenets, and that a number of you not only mentor young people but have taken it upon yourselves to support your extended families. Some of you are even rebuilding parts of the communities from which you came. But there are also so many of you who have multiple children by multiple women in multiple cities, thereby creating another generation of young people who, like many of us, barely know or see our fathers. The problem, brothers, is that we still live in an America where, despite Barack Obama being in the White House, and despite the great racial progress made since the days of Muhammad Ali, Arthur Ashe and Jim Brown, sensationalistic and negative images of Black males are more likely to make the news than a positive story.

Moreover, if you, as a professional athlete, have little or no connection to the world at large, your reality gets warped, and you truly will begin to believe the hype that you can do anything you want on any given day. Life simply does not work like that, as both Michael Vick and Plaxico Burress learned with their prison terms. For no one cares if you are a $100-million-dollar athlete or caught the game-winning touchdown in the Super Bowl; you are still a Black man in America with a target on your back. Just ask the average young Black male in any 'hood in America. What you have in common is that if you give this society the rope to hang you with, it will be used. Period. The difference is that you have a career and a life option those boys back in the 'hood would love to have. Throwing it away mindlessly is the worst kind of self-sabotage.

The fact is, brothers, because of the hip-hop and professional sports explosion of the Black male image across the American pop-culture landscape, you are more loved and more hated than ever before. Loved because people of all backgrounds live through your unbelievable athletic prowess, hated because you are a Black male with the audacity to strut and flaunt without shame. I think some of you have forgotten or are clueless to the history of racism in America as it relates to us. I understand your cool pose; I get it, because I am a Black male, and I know the historical and present-day need for us to feel powerful and validated. But if you neither know about nor can recall Jack Johnson, the first Black heavyweight champion of the world, I suggest you google his story, and see the steep price he paid for his over-the-top behavior, especially with regard to women. Now, I am certainly not suggesting you should be anything other than who you are or that you should ever bow to anyone. But what I am saying is, if you are going to be over-the-top and audacious, why not be Paul Robeson, the often-forgotten all-American athlete who went on to become a world-class concert singer, actor and human rights activist? Why not be Muhammad Ali, not just one of the greatest fighters of all time, but a man who had the bottomless courage to say he was not going fight in the Vietnam War, even though he knew he would be stripped of his heavyweight championship as a result? Why not be Jim Brown, arguably the best football player ever, who walked away from the game in his prime, and who has been a consistent voice and force in our communities, especially his work with gang members? Why not be Curt Flood, a Gold Glove-winning baseball player who, in the late 1960s, dared to challenge the St. Louis Cardinals when they decided to trade him without his consent (and despite his long tenure with the team), and his Supreme Court case literally became the foundation for the free-agent system so many athletes benefit from today? Or why not be Arthur Ashe, to this day, the first and only Black man to win tennis championships at the U.S. Open and Wimbledon?

Ashe protested apartheid in South Africa, fought for integration in America and became the personification of the Black male athlete as active citizen right up to his death.

Yes, brothers, I know the 21st century is very different from those days. But that does not mean you cannot do what those who came before you did. As Arthur Ashe documented in his important work, *A Hard Road to Glory: A History of the African-American Athlete*, you are a part of a grand tradition of Black male athletes who represented greatness on and off the field, who understood they were carrying the weight of an entire race on their backs, that their very behavior would reflect, positively or negatively, on their people.

In our times, I think often of two men who manifest this, Super Bowl-winning coach Tony Dungy and basketball legend Magic Johnson. I've had opportunities to speak with both. Mr. Dungy is retired and could easily just do his television commentary and call it a day. But he is a man in constant motion, speaking at prisons and elsewhere, and advising many athletes, including Vick and Burress, on ways to turn their lives around for the better. In our private dialogue, Mr. Dungy has talked about the fact that so many of you have not had consistent father figures in your own lives. That is why, Black male athletes, some of you truly struggle to be the men and role models we desperately need: Because you just do not know what to do, what to be, despite your fame and money. There are many men out here, like Mr. Dungy and me, who care about you. But you must be willing to ask for help, for direction, especially since so many of our young Black men look up to you and follow what you do—the good, the bad and the ugly.

Magic Johnson, likewise, is a model. He was wise enough, while still playing for the Los Angeles Lakers, to network with the wealthy business owners who frequented games and pick their brains. Thus began Magic's second career as one of the most successful Black male entrepreneurs in America. And Magic hit me with something in our phone conversation that I will never forget: more than 70 percent of football and basketball players will be broke at some point after their careers are over because of a lack of vision and proper planning. In other words, not all of you are going to get a job on ESPN or elsewhere doing commentary. If you are only living in the moment, you will get caught out there as an ex-athlete. But my hope is that most of you will wind up like NBA great Dave Bing, currently the mayor of Detroit and a long-time successful business owner in his community. We don't need any more tales of postpro careers riddled with drug and alcohol abuse, of players confessing, as Dennis Rodman recently did at his Basketball Hall of Fame induction, that they have not been good fathers, husbands, sons and men, or that they don't know how much longer they will live because their lives are in ruins.

So the ball is in your court, brothers, literally and figuratively. If you do not know what to do, I point you toward an example such as the Atlanta Hawks' Etan Thomas, who has not been afraid to use his voice to speak out against American wars overseas, to condemn Donald Trump for his attacks on President Obama, and more. I salute any ballplayer who has a charity or foundation, or has clinics for youth, no question. But what is needed now, more than ever, is a new generation of Muhammad Alis, of Jim Browns, of Arthur Ashes, of Paul Robesons and Curt Floods, sportsmen who dare to defy the odds not just when competing, but in this game we call life.

That means the headlines about you posing with guns in magazines, or punching fans in the face at summer league games must end. And it means that more of you have got to say, with conviction, "I am a man, and I want to be a man who represents the best of us with humility and honor, not the worst of who we are, fathers in our lives or not."

PART **THREE**

Let It Be...

Occupy Wall Street: The Revolution Will Be Multiplied

OCTOBER 2011
PUBLISHED IN DAILY KOS

I wasn't sure what to expect on the sunny and gusty afternoon of Wednesday, October 5, 2011, when I left a lunch meeting in the Wall Street area of Lower Manhattan, New York City. I purposely scheduled the get-together there so I could easily move from the restaurant to Zuccotti Park, on Broadway between Liberty and Cedar near Ground Zero, where protesters have been camped out for three weeks. No, they are not actually occupying Wall Street (the city and the police are making sure of that), but they are close enough, right smack in the middle of America's largest and most powerful financial district. This began this past summer when the anti-capitalist magazine *AdBusters* put out a call for Americans to occupy Wall Street on September 17th. With people's rebellions in places like Egypt, Spain, and the American state of Wisconsin still fresh in some folks' minds, seems it was only a matter of time that protests would begin to spread, like wildfire, throughout America, regardless of who is in the White House at this very moment.

I came because I am in support of the protesters, of the Occupy Wall Street movement in New York and elsewhere, for two basic reasons. One, I too have been profoundly affected, financially, by The Great Recession, and I grew up in poverty, my single mother and I, so it troubles me to the highest degree to see anyone in America suffering hardships, economic or otherwise. Secondly, I have been a political and community activist and organizer for 27 long years, since I was a teenage student and youth leader, and I've worked in all sorts of movements and mini-movements. I've organized or participated in more building takeovers, sit-ins, marches, rallies, conferences, benefits, disaster relief efforts, concerts, and political and community interventions and negotiations than I can even recall at this point. This is my life work, to help people to help themselves. Thus any time I see or hear of a critical social cause, if I am able to do so, I am going to jump right in.

It is this spirit I carried into Zuccotti Park. And what an amazing spiritual and political vibe there: People on laptops and hand-held devices typing or texting nonstop. People napping on blankets, sleeping bags, or the grass. People plucking guitar strings, blowing horns, and banging on drums and garbage cans. People having random but passionate conversations here and there about "capitalism," "democracy," "President Obama," or "the police." People sitting peacefully, in a circle, as they meditate amidst all the compelling, organic, and chaotic magic around them. People serving food to the regular protesters in the community kitchen, while other people are painting demonstration signs on strips of cardboard with captions like "Poor people did not crash the economy" or "Give me back my future." People borrowing, returning, or thumbing through books from the makeshift lending library. Everyday people, mostly younger, but certainly a number of elders, some of whom, I am sure, have in their activist resumes Civil Rights or anti-Vietnam work, or a fond memory of Woodstock. Most of the people here are White, although there is some people of color present, too. Also very clear that there are straight folks and gay folks, persons with disabilities, and persons who are war veterans, with a few wearing their camouflage-green uniforms. As I walked slowly through Zuccotti Park, from the Broadway entrance to the Trinity Place side, I thought it strangely ironic that the park's northwest corner is across the street from the old World Trade Center site. In fact Zuccotti Park was covered in debris immediately after the September 11, 2001 attacks, and subsequently was used as a staging area for recovery efforts. Kissing the sky high above Zuccotti Park now is the Freedom Tower, the 105-story edifice with a price tag of about $3 billion and counting, which will finally be opened some time in 2013.

I also thought of the fact that Lower Manhattan had once been the staging area for significant parts of the American slave trade, the importation of Africans, my people, literally creating the concept of Wall Street and the New York Stock Exchange because, well, the first stocks ever exchanged and the first global economy were enslaved Black people. As proof, not far from the Occupy Wall Street protest is the African Burial Ground, where bones of some of these Africans were discovered several years back. And before the Africans, and the European settlers, slaveholders, and colonizers, were the original owners of this land, the Native Americans. Manhattan as a word is of the Lenape language, and it means "island of many hills."

Not that any of the above would be known to the average person, or perhaps even the average protester here, but I think it important for those of us who call ourselves Americans, or human beings, or both, to be clear that nothing we do, with a structure or not, is without a context, or is ever disconnected from the history of who we are. We literally walk atop the spirits and the graves of the good and the bad that has led us to these days of protest and occupation.

We the people, that is. Therefore, this infant movement is absolutely correct in stating, loudly, "We are the 99 percent." We the American people, of diverse backgrounds, while the wealthiest 1 percent in America owns and controls 42 percent of America's wealth. You see it with the completely-out-of-control unemployment numbers and rapid freefall of America's middle class, as well as the horrific reality of America's underclass. You see it with the tax breaks and in-your-face salaries for corporations and their executives. You see it with the soaring crime rates in our communities, those crimes directly tied to financial desperation, especially in ghetto communities. You see it with students either dropping out of college due to tuition hikes and a decrease in student loans, and you see it with students with degrees on various levels that simply cannot find a job, any job. And you see it with the people sitting in court fighting foreclosure on their homes, or battling landpersons to hold onto apartments they rent.

Why this very week of the mass Occupy Wall Street protest my office has been inundated with calls, emails, and social network messages from people, everyday people, searching for work, or an apartment they can afford. One woman, a 74-year-old Brooklyn resident, is on the ledge, about to be evicted, but can only spare $800-$850 per month for rent. Her monthly social security check is $931. So she will have just $80-$130 per month to cover things like groceries, public transportation, and her prescription drugs. In the richest nation on earth it is completely inhuman and obscene that there are so many people suffering, surviving, barely, day-to-day, as images of wealth, power, and privilege are routinely thrown in our faces via our mass media culture.

So Occupy Wall Street protests in New York City and throughout America is for those of us who feel our voices and misery have been ignored. It is for those of us who believed, way down in our guts, that Barack Obama, the 2008 presidential candidate, was the change, finally, America had been waiting for. But I knew even then that that was not the case, that the best Mr. Obama could possibly be was a symbol of what was possible, but that real change only happens from the bottom up, from the people, never from the top down. That was the case with slavery and the abolitionist movement. That was the case for women and the feminist movement. That has been the case for the lesbian, bisexual, gay, and transgender community, and the gay rights movement. And that was certainly the case for Black folks and the Civil Rights Movement.

So it must be the case, now. And that is precisely why this people's "revolution" has multiplied. If you visit www.occupytogether.org, you see meet-up and actions on many levels presently happening in nearly 500 American cities. If you visit *http://wearethe99percent.tumblr.com/Introduction* you get personal testimonies from everyday people describing how tough their lives are during these times. Some mainstream media tried to ignore, distort, or even mock this movement initially, but no more. Not when celebrities like Susan Sarandon and Russell Simmons have come aboard to support, and not when 700 protesters were arrested attempting to cross the Brooklyn Bridge the other day. And not when you are dealing with a generation of young people so tech-savvy they are very clear that they are the media themselves, fully stocked with video cameras, informational websites, and even their own newspaper, *The Occupied Wall Street Journal.* This is a movement everyone, and you need to get a late pass if you are missing what is happening here. For this is historic.

At least labor unions in cities like New York and Boston get it. What made October 5th so special is that workers were present in a massive way for the first time. Some 20,000 protesters showed up, many of them belonging to my city's largest labor unions, led by their union presidents. At Foley Square, a stone's throw from the Manhattan exit of the Brooklyn Bridge, and where the long-running tv drama "Law & Order" was often filmed, nurses, teachers, and other organized labor folks swarmed to a rally and march in solidarity with the Occupy Wall Street protesters. What was most memorable is the fact that one union leader after another admitted they were simply following the lead of "these young leaders." Unions definitely remain important in New York City politics, as evidenced by the assembly line of elected officials who showed up hoping to get the obligatory photo opportunity and microphone moment. But, to me, if we are to have a truly progressive, multicultural movement in America, it Is going to demand a different kind of coalition for these times, one led by a new configuration of progressive voices, and not overwhelmed by union leaders, not overwhelmed by politicians, not overwhelmed by religious leaders, and certainly not overwhelmed by the funding of corporations or foundations (I duly noted what leaders and organizations were not in attendance because of who clearly funds their work). That old guard coalition has been happening since the Civil Rights Movement of the 1950s and 1960s and it has run its course and we must let it die a natural death. While I was certainly glad and honored to be at this union-led rally (my own mother was a long-time member of 1199SEIU in Jersey City, where I was born and raised), my heart and mind were with the people in the crowd, and back at Zuccotti Park. Later for power or ego trips, photo opps, or who can and cannot speak at a rally. This is about the people, like that 74-year-old woman my team and I are desperately trying to find an apartment she can afford. And not for nothing, we've got to support the leaders, visible or not, who are actually the voices for the people and have their pulse on the veins of the people.

For when we in leadership positions, whether we call ourselves leaders or not, and begin to think in those terms, and not in terms of our careers or our prestige or our individual or organizational agendas, then and only then do we begin to do what the Tea Party begat in 2009: a natural-birth movement led by the people, then nurtured into a full-fledged political dynamo. Part of that nurturing—and the unions made this abundantly real just by their sheer numbers—has to be the inclusion of people of color into the Occupy Wall Street movement. Until yesterday, at least in New York City, the scene was, again, mostly White sisters and brothers (yes, we all are sisters and brothers, no question). Well-meaning, yes, but good intentions do not mean you are truly progressive. Can't continue to say "We are the 99 percent" but there is not a consistent and daily picture of the rainbow coalition of America from city to city. Can't continue to say "We are the 99 percent" and your leaderless leadership (which is untrue, because someone is clearly calling the shots here, at least some of the time) is mostly White males, and not inclusive as it could be of women, of people of color, of gay sisters and brothers, and of other marginalized people as equal partners in the leadership, visible or not. Can't continue to say "We are the 99 percent" and not understand the importance of history, of our shared history of protest, of movements, and how it is going to take younger people and older people, and new activists and seasoned activists like myself, to make this into the powerful movement it can truly be, not just for a few weeks, or a few months, but for the next several years, and as needed.

And you can't continue to say "We are the 99 percent" if, eventually, there is no real agenda for the people other than a lashing out about Wall Street, about the need for jobs, or to end all wars, and on and on. Where influential Tea Party backers were both brilliant and strategic is that they saw this spontaneous thing happening and they got behind it and blew wind into the sails. So much so that there are now Tea Party political candidates within the Republican Party. And certainly Republican presidential nominee contenders who feel compelled to respond to the Tea Party national agenda.

(And, to be fair to my White sisters and brothers, Black folks and Latino folks in America in particular, two of the most in-need communities, economically, need to get off our collective behinds and fully join and co-lead the Occupy Wall Street movement. As the saying goes, either you are a part of the solution or you are a part of the problem....)

That is what we on the left, we so-called progressives or liberals or whatever we call ourselves, must do. Drive the national conversations on issues of the day in a new direction. And not as a reaction to Republicans, or the Tea Party, or right-wing conservatives, but because we understand, as a people who know change is in our hands, truly, that movements only last if you are proactive, and have a vision for what needs to happen, even while maintaining a very loose and democratic leadership structure where different voices are heard and honored.

I thought of this and more as we 20,000 strong marched down Broadway to Zuccotti Park. It was organized and disorganized, it was fast and it was slow, and it was empowering and it was frustrating. And I loved every second of the march, of the people spilling into the park, of the sense of love and peace everywhere, of the heightened intensity of the drummers, at once whipping the crowds into a frenzy, and by the same token those drums a call, spiritually, for protection of these fearless protesters. And God knows that protection was needed, because as day shook loose its clothes and became night, more New York police, on horses, on motorcycles, on foot, and in the wagons, were dispatched to the area. A security guard at a local building even told me that some plainclothes officers had come in a few times this week to go to the highest floor possible, to do surveillance on the protesters. As Russell Simmons called them, these are mostly "sweet kids." They are participating in civil disobedience, one of the grand traditions of world democracy, as taught by giants like Gandhi and Dr. King, two figures those in power love to quote when convenient. But that does not matter when the power structure of any country, be it Egypt or America, feels threatened. Or embarrassed. So when about 1000 of these protesters decided, at nightfall, to march down Broadway, to literally occupy Wall Street, they were met with the full force of the New York Police Department. About 30 were arrested and rumors immediately shot through the protest, like the stink of fresh urine on a side street wall, that a number of protesters had been beaten or maced by the police. Even a local tv crew was maced, it was said. (See http://occupywallst. org/ for more details) No matter, even more police barricades were brought out, even more police showed up, and before you knew it we were contained, like pigs in a pen, to a one-block radius on Broadway, right in front of the park. Warning sent loud and clear: you can protest, but the moment you dare to journey beyond these boundaries, we are going to stop you and arrest you.

One of my favorite chants of the movement is "Show me what democracy looks like. This is what democracy looks like." But when we beat and mace our young people for exercising their democratic rights to speak their minds and to assemble peacefully, what message are we sending to them, to ourselves, and to the world? And how are we any different, then, than Bull Connor, that infamous police chief of Birmingham Alabama, as he water-hosed and unleashed vicious barking dogs on young people during the Civil Rights era? Or leaders in foreign countries who attack their protesters for demanding democratic reform as we are doing here in the streets of America? And was it not New York City Mayor Michael Bloomberg himself, a few weeks back in a radio interview, who said there would be unrest, soon, in America, if we did not get Americans jobs? Word for word, Mr. Bloomberg stated "We have a lot of kids graduating college can't find jobs. That's what happened in Cairo. That's what happened in Madrid. You don't want those kinds of riots here."

Neither do I, Mr. Bloomberg. But, like the protesters, what I do want to see, in our nation, is economic opportunities and justice for all Americans, not just for the privileged few. And I am clear that you cannot tease people about the unlimited possibilities of America then when they decide they want to have it, tell them no, we were not being serious. Where this movement goes from here is anyone's guess. Maybe it is simply suppose to be a space where the disillusioned and disgusted can finally make their voices heard. Or maybe it will be the progressive, multicultural movement I want to see, that I feel America so badly needs, in this 21st century. No matter what happens, no matter where this goes, it is so evident, more than ever and as was said during the Civil Rights Movement, that the leadership we've been waiting for is us...

In Defense of Ashley Judd

APRIL 2011
PUBLISHED IN HUFFINGTON POST

Ashley Judd is a very courageous woman. I am not referring to her work as a global ambassador for YouthAids, or her efforts to end poverty and sexual violence in underdeveloped nations overseas, or even her journey here in America as an actress, mother, daughter of a country music star, and avid supporter of Barack Obama's 2008 presidential campaign, animal rights, and equality for women. No, none of that.

Ms. Judd is fearless because she wears her life and her feelings on her chest, bare, in plain sight, and has written a stunning new memoir, "All That is Bitter and Sweet," which discusses, with rawness and candor, her being sexually abused as a child by a grown man. We as Americans are deceiving ourselves if we do not think various forms of gender violence against women and girls is not at epidemic proportions, because it is. Just ask your mother, grandmother, sister, niece, aunt, female friends, women co-workers or classmates, girlfriend, wife, or partner, and I guarantee you someone in that group will have a story similar to Ashley Judd's either as girls, or during their adult years.

It is for this reason alone that Ms. Judd's new book is so timely, and so necessary. April is Sexual Assault Awareness Month in America and, sadly, as I do a quick scan, right this moment, of New York headlines just from the past 2-3 days, there is the Manhattan man who stabbed his girlfriend to death, and the Brooklyn man who choked his girlfriend until she likewise died. Simply imagine the reported and unreported tales of American women and girls being abused, molested, stalked, street harassed, raped, beaten, choked, stabbed, shot, set on fire, or murdered each and every single day. Then imagine these same acts in nations across the globe, each and every single day. Thus, Ashley Judd's very personal saga is for women and girls in America, overseas, everywhere, whose voices have not been heard. Or roundly dismissed or ignored.

As a writer myself, I know that the telling of one's story is about healing, and transformation. And making a pact with one's self not to tolerate certain kinds of abuses or behaviors ever again. And if one has been wounded, the way Ms. Judd was badly wounded as a child, one will, in adulthood, once one has found one's voice, become a drum major for justice, a truth-teller. Which easily explains why Ms. Judd has crisscrossed America, and many a foreign country, taking on the difficult causes of everyday people. She is that everyday person herself in so many ways, from the sexual assault as a child, to the constant moving about (she literally attended 13 different schools by the time she graduated from high school), to the splintered relationships with her parents. Her story is our story and we know it well.

Unfortunately, that Ms. Judd is a famous Hollywood actress today means that a different kind of attention is being paid to her memoir. The good part is that she has an instant platform to discuss topics like gender violence. The bad part is that, in our very dumbed down, social network-obsessed society, it becomes quite easy and convenient for words to be taken out of context or, worse yet, not read at all, and just passed around, one tweet and facebook post at a time, until what Ms. Judd wrote very eloquently in her memoir is completely distorted.

Case in point are the very heated attacks Ms. Judd has received for saying, in her book, that "most rap and hiphop music—with its rape culture and insanely abusive lyrics and depiction of girls and women as 'ho's'—is the contemporary sound track of misogyny."

If anyone had bothered to read pages 58-62 of Ms. Judd's memoir, then they would know she put into context not only how she was asked to be a part of YouthAids, where hiphop icons P. Diddy and Snoop Dogg were serving as spokespersons, but you get her evident grappling, as a sexual abuse survivor, as a feminist, and as a human being, of making peace with working with them, and 50 Cent, too, in spite of her real and righteous feelings about gender violence. And why wouldn't she? For example, besides a career weighted with lyrics calling women all sorts of derogatory terms, Snoop once showed up at the MTV Video Music Awards with two women on dog leashes. What woman, with any level of self-respect, would want to be associated with that definition of manhood?

Instead what we who call ourselves men, or hiphop heads, or whatever, have done is myopically label Ashley Judd as "racist," "a dumb White woman," and other terms which are simply not printable in this space. As a man, as a Black man, as a heterosexual Black man, who has been deeply involved in both hiphop culture and the hiphop industry for 30 years, I was not offended by Ms. Judd's words.

That's because I believe in speaking the truth always: America in general has always been a male-dominated, sexist nation. This is nothing new. Hiphop did not create sexism, misogyny, abuse, disrespect, a culture of rape, or violence against women. No. Those behavioral patterns go back to the days of the Pilgrims, the so-called founding fathers, and slavery, as if we are to be historically and culturally accurate.

But because hiphop has been the dominant cultural expression since at least the 1980s, in America, in the world, it has also come to embody many of the worst aspects of male privilege and domination. In other words, if you are born a male in this nation, unless there was some sort of intervention at some point in your life teaching you that women and girls are your equals, that love is preferable to hate, mindless ego, and reckless competition, that nonviolence trumps violence and warfare any day, guess what kind of man you, we, are more than likely primed to be?

Moreover, given that hiphop was created by working-class Black and Latino urban males, we have been the face of this cultural juggernaut in spite it being embraced by multicultural people worldwide (and barely controlled by us in terms of the mass production and distribution of words, sounds, and images). So when Ms. Judd declared hiphop had a "rape culture" many of us went off, because our interpretation is that she is saying Black and Latino males are the ones doing this to women and girls. Of course that is not the case.

And that is precisely where the thorny dynamic of White folks and Black folks in America once again crashes into that concrete wall called American history. We each bring to the table an airport full of baggage and what should be routine conversations and the exchange of ideas turn into mean-spirited broadsides with folks puffing out their chests and declaring beef over here! The result, ever more, is we surely cannot hear nor decipher what the other is saying. And while race takes center stage once again via the Ashley Judd episode the matter of sexism, of violence and reckless disregard for the female body, is tossed aside as if it is a non-issue. Yes, once again, the views of a woman does not matter is what we are essentially saying by responding as we've done on the internet. It is not just because Ms. Judd is White, either. I have seen the same harsh reactions to Black, Latina, and Asian women who would dare offer a critique of sexist behavior in a public forum.

And I seriously doubt Ashley Judd has spent so much time, energy, and a good deal of her own resources in Africa if she were, indeed, a card-carrying racist. She is not. She is a genuinely caring human being as evidenced by a life dedicated as much to public service as it is to her acting career. I think the only thing Ms. Judd is probably guilty of here is being an outsider and not understanding the totality of hiphop, its mores, its customs, its defiant swagger. Particularly that of us Black and Latino males for whom hiphop is everything in a world where we feel we are forever battling for our identities and our pieces of the American dream, real or imagined. But you do not move to destroy someone because of what they may not know. You take the time, if you have any sense of humanity, to teach. Always.

I am a hiphop head for life, since my days dancing on streets and at clubs and writing graffiti on walls; to my days as a writer for Vibe magazine and curating the first exhibit on hiphop history at the Rock and Roll Hall of Fame; to my current task of writing a biography, the next several years, on the life of Tupac Shakur. So I know there is a difference between hiphop culture, which I represent, and the hiphop industry, which is what Ashley Judd is referencing in her book.

And we'd be lying to ourselves, hiphop heads or not, if we actually could say, with straight faces, that hiphop culture has not been severely undermined, turned inside out, and made into an industry that promotes some of the most horrific images of women and men, that encourages oversexualization and materialism, that pushes anti-intellectualism and a brand of manhood that seems only to exist if one is engaging in the most destructive forms of violence and degrading of one's self, and of others. That is not hiphop. That is called a minstrel show, circa the 21st century. And if you really love something the way I love that some thing called hiphop, then we would be honest about it and not go on ego trips attacking an Ashley Judd for having the courage to say what we should be saying ourselves.

That enough is enough of this madness, that it is no longer acceptable to say our culture is just reflecting what is going on in our communities. Art is not just to reflect what is happening. Art, at its best, is also about dialoguing about and correcting the ugliness in our communities. That will not happen if art is just as ugly as real life, if we are at a point where we cannot tell real life from the staged life.

For sure, Ms. Judd mentions this in her book when she talks about 50 Cent offstage, how professional and polite he was, then the moment he took the stage out came the hyper-masculinity, the bravado, the posturing, the manufactured character. Rather than curse out or disparage Ashley Judd, I think we should instead ask ourselves who we are, truly, in these times, and why so many of us continue to have our identities programmed and directed by record labels and radio and video channels under the illusion of keeping it 100 percent real? Real for whom, and at what cost to our communities?

Back in the 1990s, when I was writing for Vibe, I did an interview with the late C. Delores Tucker, an older Black woman who led a crusade against what she thought were indecent rap lyrics. I was so much younger emotionally and in terms of basic common sense, and did everything I could to make Ms. Tucker look like a buffoon in the printed interview. I really regret that because these women, the real leaders on our planet, are right. Why should it be acceptable to tolerate any culture, be it hiphop, rock, jazz, reality tv, video games, or certain kinds of Hollywood films, that create a space that says it is okay, normal, to denigrate women and girls with words and images?

To his credit, hiphop mogul Russell Simmons provided Ashley Judd a space, on globalgrind.com, to squash any so-called hiphop beef, a term I wish we hiphop heads would discard once and for all. Ms. Judd apologized for not choosing some of her words better, but she held firm, as she should have, around the issue of violence against women and girls.

On his Twitter feed Russell said "Real talk, if women were empowered we would protect the environment, the animals and have much less war." But women's empowerment, Russell, and the dismantling of male domination, will not happen if we men and boys do not become active agents in ending any behavior that blocks and destroys the natural evolution of girls into the powerful women they ought to be. And, Russell, as you say elsewhere in your Twitter feed, it is not an argument on whether rappers are less or more sexist than their parents or ministers. The issue is that sexism, period, is wrong, and we need to put as much vigor into ending it as we do in battling racism, anti-Semitism, homophobia, classism, religious intolerance, or any other kind of oppression and discrimination. Debating degrees of something is just not the way.

Furthermore, any males out there who have a daughter or daughters need to ponder this very seriously. Even if you are not the kind of man who engages in foul language or abusive or violent behavior toward women or girls, do you say anything when it is happening around you, by your male friends or colleagues or family members? And how would you feel if these kinds of things were being said or done to your mother, to your daughter?

We need to understand, finally, that Ashley Judd is someone's daughter, too, and but for the grace of the universe, some serious healing work, and, again, an insurmountable desire to live, and be, she is able to tell her story and help others. The worst thing we could ever do, as men, as human beings, is to not listen when someone is telling her or his truth.

For in one's personal truth are lessons for us all.

Open Letter to Mayor Michael Bloomberg of New York

NOVEMBER 2011
PUBLISHED IN HUFFINGTON POST

Dear Mayor Bloomberg:

I was awakened in the wee hours of this morning by texts and calls from friends and associates distraught that Occupy Wall Street protestors were being forcibly removed from Zuccotti Park in Lower Manhattan. Even more troubling is that you chose to make a mockery of the First Amendment of our United States Constitution by not only evicting the peaceful activists, but also by blocking media outlets from recording the police raid. This is America, Mr. Bloomberg, a nation that through much effort, tears, blood, and, yes, deaths, has evolved from a slaveholding country that also destroyed much of Native American culture, to one where women, people of color, the lesbian, gay, bisexual, and transgender community, the physically challenged, Jews, Muslims, White ethnics from places like Ireland and Italy, and so many others have been able to gain some measure of freedom

KEVIN POWELL

and democracy. We are not the nation we ought to be, yet, but we are also not the nation we once were, either. We do that history, and ourselves, a great disservice when we in leadership positions resort to tactics used to deny freedom and democracy, in the old America of Jim Crow laws, in the old South Africa of apartheid.

As I watched the amateur video made of the raid online this morning, I got very choked up. I am a big supporter of Occupy Wall Street because it speaks directly to my history as a Black person in America. The occupation is nothing more than the bus boycotts, freedom rides, and sit-ins of the Civil Rights era. The nonviolent approach harkens back to the principles of Dr. King, borrowed, of course, from the great Indian leader Gandhi. The use of technology to spread the Occupy Wall Street messages is no different than how W.E.B. DuBois, Marcus Garvey, and other visionaries used the media at their disposal in their day to communicate with the masses. So when we choose to walk down the path of repression, of removing and silencing those who would speak out, Mr. Mayor, we are saying that we are choosing to be on the wrong side of history. That we are choosing to be in bed with the devil, instead of on the side of God, of the noble promises of our America.

As I said, I am a supporter of the Occupy Wall Street movement, here in New York City, and across America. I have been a part of many rallies and marches the past two months. I have spent much time talking and listening to participants, at Zuccotti Park, at planning meetings, and in private one-on-one sessions with some of the leadership. They are mostly good and

decent Americans and I have not witnessed a movement like
this since the anti-apartheid protests of the 1980s when I was a
college student. It is the same energy, the same sense of purpose,
and the same fire-in-belly belief that what they are doing is
right. They are not anti-American. They are not anti-business.
They are not anti-wealthy folks. They are not anti-police. They
are not anti-you, Mr. Mayor. They, we, merely want to see our
nation be a place where people, regardless of race, class, gender,
sexual orientation, physical ability, religion, or educational
level can have an opportunity to have an opportunity; to not
struggle to get or keep a job or career; to not struggle to pay
for an education which should be our birthright; to not suffer
through housing woes, including foreclosures; to not have to
spend our entire lives in debt, broke, or broken spiritually and
emotionally because of our finances.

But what message are we sending, Mayor Bloomberg,
when we come like the thief in the night to remove people
by extreme force? What message are we sending when we
inhumanly destroy a community built to show what democracy
can look like in our era? How condescending and nearsighted
are we to state these people are dirty and unfocused, that they
somehow are more of a public nuisance than certain banks and
corporations that have wrecked the lives of so many Americans?
How arrogant are we to assume, just because we may have a
certain financial background, status, or title, to think we are
above relearning lessons of democracy at various points in our
American lives? And how can we ever again say it was not right
for militaries in Middle Eastern and North African nations to

crack down on the democracies there, then we turn around and do the same on our own shores, only months later, and to our own children, to our own people?

Mayor Bloomberg, you said on your weekly radio show, several weeks ago, that it was inevitable for Americans to take to the streets because of the state of our economy. But is the solution to beat these people back with batons and gloved fists, or is the solution to listen to their voices, hear their concerns, and figure out a way, together, for us as a people, all people, to transform America for these times and beyond?

I know somewhere in your person, Mayor Bloomberg, you have a soul and a moral conscience. You are going to have to ask yourself, billionaire or not, Mayor of New York City or not, whose side you are on, because the Occupy Wall Street movement is here to stay, and will only get bigger and stronger when leaders like you attack the protestors, as you've done. Justice, Mr. Bloomberg, is not on the side of those who would misuse and abuse their power. Justice is, forever, on the side of those who would even sacrifice their own bodies because they believe so deeply in their cause. Those are the kind of people and the kind of Americans I stand with, Mayor Bloomberg. Those are the kind of people I know, from their tents, blankets, and makeshift occupied communities, will do for America exactly what those Civil Rights workers did with their shoes, overalls, songs of freedom, and voter registration cards a generation ago. And so it shall be, and so it shall be—

Heaven Hell Dave Chappelle

MAY 2006
PUBLISHED IN ESQUIRE

N o one can imagine what it is like to be Dave Chappelle on this very night. No one. Here he is, the comic genius of America, curbside at the aristocratic Beverly Hills hotel Raffles L'Ermitage, Hollywood's new celebrity magnet, pacing back and forth, habitually fielding phone calls and thumbing through his BlackBerry and inhaling Camel after Camel as he anticipates a ride to the 2006 Grammy Awards from Chris Tucker, a longtime friend and funnyman frat brother. Disrobed of his customary hip-hop uniform of sagging, ballooned jeans, agitprop T-shirt, tennis shoes (as they say in the Midwest), and a charcoal-black hoodie, Chappelle is wearing a brown pinstripe suit, a crisp white shirt, a coffee-colored tie, and tan leather shoes--very much resembling a young man in a courtroom awaiting his fate. And appearing very uncomfortable, as if he is in the wrong costume for a morality play in which he is the reluctant lead actor. Certainly, it is hard to say what, precisely, is running through Dave Chappelle's mind on this muggy February evening

KEVIN POWELL

in southern California. On the surface, at least, he is at once excited and mad nervous.

Excited because tonight, for the first time since his well-documented exit from his hit Comedy Central variety program in May 2005, the critically acclaimed "Chappelle's Show," he will be in the midst of a constellation of entertainment heavies. In fact, Chappelle will introduce the musical tribute to Sly Stone, the reclusive soul and funk visionary who has not performed in public since Ronald Reagan was president. Stone, as hearsay has it, had grown to despise the limelight and opted out for a less demanding life. The irony is not lost on Chappelle, who too made himself scarce when he became unhappy with the executives overseeing his wildly popular franchise and bolted, last May, midway through the shooting schedule, to Africa. So wildly popular and cultish is "Chappelle's Show" that it has broken a number of DVD sales records, in spite of being on the air for only two full seasons to date. And "Chappelle's Show" has been called a singular juggernaut in the annals of American television comedy, a cable show up there alongside "Rowan and Martin's Laugh-In," "The Carol Burnett Show," "Saturday Night Live," and "In Living Color." But Dave Chappelle has been paying the price of the fame ticket for walking away from a deal worth upwards of $50 million. His every public move–on "Oprah," on "Inside the Actors Studio," as he bikes down Xenia Avenue in his hometown of Yellow Springs, Ohio--has been dissected, applauded, and, yeah, ridiculed; his paper-thin sanity has been questioned and shredded; his virtual body bandied about by a mosh pit of hands and handlers who've come and gone; and his rubbery soul, the one that believes very quietly yet very deeply in Allah, in the religion of Islam, has been deformed by media, fans, and the player haters. There are Web sites set up by Chappelle worshipers and fanatics on which Chappelle can do no wrong; and, likewise, there are sites proposing bizarre and warped conspiracy theories on why Chappelle pulled the plug on himself. It seems, these days, if Dave Chappelle merely catches a cold, it winds up in the media or on the Internet.

So it is understandable that tonight Dave Chappelle is nervous. He does not know how his peers will receive him, if at all, for he has done something that is unthinkable for the rich and recognizable: He has openly rejected the glamour, the mystique, the fast money, and the fast life. Chappelle, as he will say again and again over the nine days I spend with him, simply wants freedom--the freedom to make art the way he feels it should be made; the freedom to live wherever he pleases; the freedom to control his own destiny, his own identity. So even something as minor as the script he has been handed to study for the Sly Stone monologue becomes a raging internal battle for him. These are not my words. I would never say something like this. Is it weird that I am the one introducing the Sly tribute? No, Chappelle is not going to do it. There is more pacing, another drag on another cigarette, sidewalk consultation with his publicist. Okay, I will do it, but I will change it, improvise, make it feel natural, proudly identifying with Stone's legacy of doing things his way.

As Chappelle rotates the script, like a diploma, between his long brown fingers and walks back and forth once more, Chris Tucker finally arrives. He is not in a limousine nor in a Town

Car but in a bus, a great big tour bus, complete with bodyguard, television set, DVD player, booming stereo system, fully loaded refrigerator, washer and dryer, and bedroom. Not yet dressed for the Grammys himself, Tucker peeps Dave Chappelle's pinstripe suit from head to toe, circles him like a tailor assessing a client, squints his eyes to gain the correct focus, cocks his head the way they do in his native Georgia, then exclaims, with that whiny megaphone of a voice of his, "Man, Chappelle, you look like a preacher who done lost his congregation!"

There is a comfort level that Chappelle feels on this bus with Chris Tucker. It is a safe space before the rush of his evening to come. As Earth, Wind & Fire's "Fantasy" wafts from the stereo system, Tucker and Chappelle engage in the sort of easy, carefree banter reminiscent of childhood pals. Chappelle does not have to explain to Tucker what cross he is bearing, because Tucker understands instinctively. They met in the early 1990s, a period that witnessed a renaissance in American comedy and Black American humor, thanks to what Eddie Murphy had wrought throughout the 1980s: the comedian as rock star. And if you were a Black stand-up comic, you automatically had that infrared light trained on your forehead, targeting you as the next Eddie Murphy. Chris Rock had it. So did Martin Lawrence, so did Cedric the Entertainer, Bernie Mac, Damon Wayans, Chris Tucker, and, yes, Dave Chappelle. Tucker had his mind-boggling explosion first, becoming a box-office smash and multimillion-dollar star in the process. And today Chappelle is there, or somewhere near there, and it has been a tremendously complex adjustment. As he would say on another day: "It's like someone saying, 'You're the CEO of a $50 million company--good luck!' And then kinda leaving you to your own devices. I've been a comedian since I was fourteen. But I've never really been a CEO."

Tucker and Chappelle disappear to the back of the bus to converse in solemn, hushed tones. It would become a pattern throughout Grammy night, of Chappelle huddling with the likes of Chuck D, Jamie Foxx, Stevie Wonder. You get the impression that Chappelle is both fighting and finding himself amid all the impromptu discussions. Then the Tucker bus barrels into the parking lot of the Staples Center. When it is made known that Chris Tucker and Dave Chappelle are on board, the atmosphere becomes electric. The two old buddies say their goodbyes for the moment (Tucker has to don a suit) and pledge to cross paths at Prince's annual post-Grammy bash in a few hours. In one breath he is relaxed and hysterical with Tucker on the bus, and in the next breath Chappelle, as his loping strides stamp the pavement, is suddenly taut, and in dire need of another cigarette. He fumbles inside his jacket and pants pockets. Light. Drag. Eyes flicker open and shut. Exhale. Sigh. Okay, he is ready for that close-up.

Passing through the celebrity entrance, Chappelle is taken aback by the instantaneous and hearty adulation he receives from parking attendants, security personnel, greeters, laborers, sound technicians, and stagehands. Inside, as he snakes his way through the hordes offstage, there are pounds on the back, firm handshakes and hugs, and several cries of "Welcome back!" "Are you okay?" and "We missed you!" There is Madonna with an entourage of what seems like fifty. "I think she gave me a dirty look," Chappelle says impishly, although I don't see Madonna see Chappelle as her cloud of bodies whisks her by the ooohs and aaahs. There is Carlos Santana and Paul McCartney. There is Sting and Jay-Z. There is Green Day, led by frontman Billie Joe Armstrong, running like unabashed groupies up to Chappelle for a picture, testifying to him how much they admire his work. There are the youth, black, white, it does not matter, here with parents or whomever, screaming--screaming--as Chappelle saunters by, begging for autographs and photos, chanting Chappelle catchphrases that have become a part of the American vocab—" I'm Rick James, bitch!" Chappelle is at once tickled and embarrassed by this ruckus, stops for every single person, famous or not, who says his name, then finally makes a beeline to the rostrum to do his Sly Stone bit. There is lengthy applause and an appreciative air. Chappelle basks in it for a brief second, then says, "The only thing harder than leaving show business is coming back." One minute is a lifetime in the entertainment industry, and Chappelle, done and satisfied, swiftly retires to the sound-equipment loading zone, grabs a squat on a golf cart, and lights up a Camel as he digests this Grammy affair--his triumphant return, on his terms--with his publicist.

As he sits there pulling on his cigarette, I rewind to the Dave Chappelle I met in 1993 in New York City via my then girlfriend, an actress who'd attended Washington's illustrious Duke Ellington School of the Arts with him. Then fast-forward to the last time I saw Dave in person, Saturday, September 18, 2004, when he staged and filmed *Dave Chappelle's Block Party* in the very nook of Brooklyn where the late rapper the Notorious B. I. G. had grown up. On that rainy September day, Dave Chappelle was, so I thought, at the apex of his personal joy around his successful show, and very much at ease with his spanking-new notoriety. Dave swam through the crowd, soaking in its love for him, reaching for people as they were grabbing at him. He chastised employees who were taking too long to permit fans through the barricades to see this free concert featuring him, Kanye West, Erykah Badu, and other personalities; and Chappelle made it a point to bring residents on buses, at his own expense, from his Yellow Springs community in Ohio to Brooklyn for this Woodstock-meets-Wattstax gathering. Indeed, Chappelle had financed much of the day, including the film crew, from his own bank account. It was surreal, truthfully, to view Dave Chappelle in this light, because it had been a long time coming.

I remember being at the Boston Comedy Club in Greenwich Village and watching this tall, bone-thin young man with the contagious, toothy smile, the deep-socket, saucerlike eyes, and the perfectly oval head atop a twig of a neck wreck the mic, the stage, and the room like an old-school rapper. Only nineteen at the time, Chappelle was nicknamed by Whoopi Goldberg "the Kid." Even then there was a razor-sharp racial consciousness to Chappelle's material--he had a keen eye for that gray area between social satire and pop culture--and on that occasion I was lucky to witness something very special. Here was the classic working-class intellect of Charlie Chaplin's conniving tramp, the jazzy, in-your-face audacity of Lenny Bruce's birth-of-cool bebopper, and the gut-bucket, bluesy aches and pains of Richard

Pryor's dead-on mimes, all in one. There are comedians who have to work at being funny, but Chappelle seemed born to it. Back at the Grammys, Chappelle discards another cigarette (I've lost count at this point), the show is over, and we head out of the Staples Center to Prince's party. As the rented black SUV nudges its way around West Hollywood, Chappelle is relieved. "I didn't know what to expect, even though I swear Madonna gave me a dirty look." Laughter pops inside the SUV as we arrive at Prince's mansion. And what a mansion it is. Tall iron gates. Beige granite with the numbers of the address deliberately jumbled. A swarm of chiseled, no-neck security men. Parking valets zigzagging from vehicle to vehicle. A Gothic doorman with black eyeliner, black fingernail polish, and a black tongue ring, standing there with a guest list on a clipboard. "Is this a club or Prince's home?" Chappelle asks no one in particular. Dave Chappelle is not on the sheet, but he's admitted after Prince himself is told who is waiting outside the iron gate. A shuttle van is sent down to ride us up the hill to Prince's palace. It is a thirteen-second excursion we could have done by foot.

If Dave Chappelle is hyped to be here, he does not show it, and as we go by two hostesses at the colossal threshold to Prince's home, one of them says to Chappelle wryly, "You need to thank Prince for letting you in." No reaction from Chappelle, but he does make it a point to spot Prince, promptly, and walks right over to thank him for his hospitality. Although Chappelle stands nearly six feet and is long and wiry, it is the elfin Prince, in natty out?t--a blue blazer, white slacks, white shoes--who is the Goliath in this instance. Dig if you will this picture: Chappelle's a kid all of a sudden, the pubescent Dave who worshiped Prince in the 1980s. His gaunt face is tight and nervous, and his gleaming eyes bounce like ping-pong balls from the Purple One's face to the hardwood floor. But ain't Dave Chappelle famous, too? And for sure, dues-paying members of the fame club are omnipresent and accounted for at this joint: Mariah Carey, Alicia Keys, Jeremy Piven from HBO's "Entourage," and Morris Day and the Time, the headliners for the evening.

But rather than indulge in the festivities, Chappelle retreats outdoors to the patio area, to a double-back chair positioned against a back wall next to one of four bars operating this evening. Swirling around him are servers feverishly rotating finger foods, music royalty like Carey, Jermaine Dupri, and Common powwowing near the kitchen, industry check writers making deals over cocktails, industry wannabes swapping business cards and phony pleasantries, party crashers whispering, pointing, and stargazing, and Morris Day and his sidekick, Jerome, working the crowd into a sweaty frenzy as the band whips through its classic songs like "777-9311." But Dave Chappelle sits, and sits, and sits, from round midnight to after 4:00 A.M., methodically smoking his cigarettes, sipping on spring water, eating the cupcakes floating on the server trays, and engaging anyone who sits down next to him. He looks uncomfortable in this scene. Indeed, slouching low in the chair, his spine curved into a tight knot, Dave Chappelle looks as if he is hiding: hiding from his peers, hiding from the attention, hiding from that part of himself that is a major star.

After all, Dave Chappelle is really just a simple Midwestern homeboy, with uncomplicated, wholesome Midwestern values, who happens to have a bottomless well of talent. Through the course of the evening, from Raffles L'Ermitage to the Grammy Awards to his cushiony seat as a spectator at Prince's party, Chappelle seems to be having an out-of-body experience. It is him, but then again it is not him at all. Or, rather, as he says to me during one of the many hours we are there with Prince and company, "Man, I don't drink, I don't dance, I don't party--this ain't really my thing." Problem is that when you become an icon, as Dave Chappelle has become, it does not matter what you want. The people want you. And so Dave Chappelle is trying to understand how to give the universe what it demands of someone with his calling while keeping some version of himself for himself. And that is why he refuses to do a Hollywood shuffle, ever. What is evident, here at Prince's mansion, as his bottom remains pasted to that chair, is that he is not going to budge, not now, not for just anyone.

At the close of the night, Chappelle finally leaps from his seat when he eyeballs music impresario Quincy Jones. Like a little boy, he shyly introduces himself, but of course Jones knows who he is. When Chappelle was a student at Duke Ellington, Jones came to screen the documentary film "Listen Up," brought copies for the school, and books of the same title, for the entire student body. Chappelle said that Jones came into the auditorium while he was onstage doing comedy, and that goosebumps covered his body. "You never really stop looking at these people as how you saw them as a child, as a kid," Chappelle says in reference to Prince, to Quincy Jones, to Eddie Murphy, his boyhood idol.

BARACK OBAMA, RONALD REAGAN, AND THE GHOST OF DR. KING

"I mean, man, I love them."

And they love Dave Chappelle, but Chappelle truly believes, in his heart, he is not part of the club. "Look at where I live, man. I don't have that kind of connection with me being famous. Fame for me is like a place, a country I'm taking a tour through. You just don't walk around feeling like 'I'm a goddamn star.' You walk around feeling like you."

Chappelle, as it turns out, stays too long in Los Angeles. He is moving in too many directions, is too unsure of himself in that environment, too cryptic about those phone calls he is retrieving from lawyers, colleagues, whomever, which leave him one minute elated and the next very obviously on the edge of dismay and anger. And when he ultimately has enough of the sun, the shades, the posturing, Dave Chappelle decides he is going back to Ohio, to be with his family, to detach himself, for a few days at any rate, from the showbiz machine.

Yellow Springs is a sleepy outpost in southwest Ohio, population hovering near four thousand, and address of the ultraliberal Antioch College, where Dave Chappelle's late father was once a professor. Everyone seems to know everyone, everyone speaks, nods a head, or proffers a wink, a peace sign, or a thumbs-up. The Underground Railroad, that gateway to liberation for escaped slaves from the South, ran through some of Yellow Springs' older dwellings, with secret hideouts still intact. And it is in this mostly White community of artists, intellectuals, and activists that you can get a supersized cup of espresso or herbal tea at Dino's Cappuccinos, a vegetarian meal at the Sunrise Cafe, and be Dave Chappelle, regular American citizen. Practically from the hour he hits the pavement on Xenia Avenue, the hub of this remote village, Chappelle is rejuvenated.

There he is borrowing a random kid's skateboard and darting, skillfully, between moving and parked cars. There he is chasing one of his two teeny sons, like a giant monster, into his family-pack Toyota SUV. There he is teasing and making faces at his lovely wife, a petite Filipina from Brooklyn. And there he is, in a montage of scenes, with his brother, home for a spell from his postgraduate religious studies in California; with his sister, clad, like Chappelle's brother, in full Muslim garb; and with his mother, a prominent African-American-studies scholar and the first black woman in this country to be named, in 1981, a Unitarian Universalist minister. And his mother, too, is a Muslim.

For Dave Chappelle, there is a tranquillity about this town, where no one probes his or his family's faith or personal lives; where no one asks for an autograph or photo but once during the five days I am here with him; where an employee at Yellow Springs' lone movie theater shrugs her shoulders indifferently when told, by Chappelle himself, that "Dave Chappelle's Block Party" will be coming soon; where he, in spite of the change in environment, blazes cigarette after cigarette like a fireplace burning log after log. Except here in Yellow Springs, his lips do not clamp down as hard on the cigarette, and the sucking in of nicotine is not as resolute as it was in Los Angeles.

But Dave Chappelle is still not entirely at peace. And he is finding himself incapable of pausing to talk. I don't think I can do this, he says. In a way, he still seems to be fleeing

whatever he was fleeing when he left for Africa. He is in constant
motion, pacing up and down Xenia Avenue on the cell phone
and thumbing, as usual, through the BlackBerry. And each time
we settle into Dino's or the Sunrise to talk, it is not long before
he is up again, his mind and soul so tormented, it appears, that
he is not even sure enough of who he is at this very moment
to talk about himself. It is not until I am here for two days that
we climb into Chappelle's Toyota and begin driving in circles
around Yellow Springs, during sunlight and late at night for
hours, for three straight days, and he begins to speak.

It comes in a swirl, impressionistic and crackling funny,
and Chappelle's reticence is swept away in a cascade of words
and turns of the steering wheel. "I got crib memories. I can
remember people looking down at me when I was in the crib.
I have a loooong memory. Perfect for holding grudges!... In
the last year, I started getting perspective on how my machine
works—my joke machine, or my creative process. Which is at
odds with how this business works to some degree, 'cause I'm a
complainer by nature, which is just part of my machine... I left in
pre-crack Washington and came back in post-crack Washington,
so I got the before-and-after picture. It was literally jolting, like,
what the fuck happened? My freshman year of high school, over
five hundred kids my age were murdered...Miles Davis said it
was his fantasy to choke a white man, but he made some of
the best music he ever made with Gil Evans. It's like artists can
transcend race like nobody can... I finished my first show and
the crowd went fuckin' nuts. All the comics were in a lounge,
and they go, 'How old are you?' And I said, 'I'm fourteen.' And

they said, 'Goddamn.' ... Years later I was pulling up to a hotel in D. C. I had a nice car at the time. And I get out and this old White man is the valet, with a red sweater on. And I hand him the keys, he hands me a ticket, and he goes, 'That's not my car.' He goes, 'I wish it was my car.' And I go, 'Oh, yeah, that's nice, thanks.' So then, finally I realized—I'm thinking he's the valet, and he's thinking I'm the valet. But I said, 'Well, at least I was thinking that 'cause you have on black slacks and a red sweater.' He was thinking that 'cause I have Black skin [laughs], 'cause nothing about me was lookin' like a valet... I'm the first person in my family that wasn't a slave that didn't go to college. My great-grandparents were slaves and still went to college... Suffering and humans go hand in hand. Look at comedy. It's dominated by Black people and Jewish people. That is American comedy. And if blacks and Jews didn't do comedy, we'd be relying on the Irish. 'Cause they were the next funniest thing... The only movie they kept offering me over and over was fuckin' "Soul Plane." They kept giving me the script and I'd say, 'I passed on this script.' And it would just keep coming back. 'No, I don't want to do Soul Plane!'... Maybe the pendulum is swinging back and people want entertainment that has a little more substance. Dude, the number-one song on the radio is 'Shake That Laffy Taffy.' There's a group of people out there that rebel against that. Like, this is the shit you're cramming down my throat? 'Shake That Laffy Taffy'?... Genius is such a grandiose term. I didn't do it all by myself. Sometimes I get credit for things I don't really deserve. And other times I don't get credit for things that I do think I deserve... This phrase kept coming up: It's not personal, it's just business. If you ever hear a White man say that, even if you are White, run for your motherfucking life.When a person tells you something's not personal, it's just business, that means some ice-cold shit might be about. . . . I want to, like, play Sambo, but I want to give those characters some depth. No, just kidding. No, I'm just kidding, man... You know, nowadays it ain't easy to be anygoddamnbody."

And Dave Chappelle flows so freely now, on and on, his Toyota SUV seemingly a safe space, a therapist's couch. Round and round Yellow Springs until I have the town memorized and we're mainlining the coffee. Until, on one particular side street, Chappelle presses the brakes and prods the vehicle along and mutters somberly, "That is where my father is buried." It is a quaint, one-story stucco home. His dad's grave is in the backyard, and his widow, Chappelle's stepmother, a white woman, is home right now. We drive on, and I think back to when I first met Chappelle, how he'd introduced me to a young white man whom he described as "my brother." Today it makes sense. It was his stepmother's son.

It is this sort of double consciousness into which Dave Chappelle was born in Washington, D. C., on August 24, 1973, in the shimmering shadow of Watergate and Vietnam, amid civil-rights-era residue, a precocious boy who, by his own account, had a very happy childhood. His father, "a hippie," held down a corporate job for years as a statistician but was really a lover of music, of art, of books, a man with an IQ of 185. His mother, the more overtly rebellious of his parents, once worked for the revolutionary Patrice Lumumba in the Congo and was an independent thinker and dedicated intellectual, constantly reinventing herself in the pursuit of a better grasp of life. Though together only for the initial brushstrokes of Dave Chappelle's life, the two shared duties in shaping the mind of their youngest child. "Growing up, I knew kids who lived with both their parents that didn't have as close a relationship with their parents.

"I grew up in Silver Spring, Maryland. We were like the broke Huxtables. There were books around the house, everybody was educated to a college level. We used to have a picture of Malcolm X in Ghana. Last Poets records. We were poor but we were cultured."

And there was the home education money could never buy: little Chappelle sitting among adults as they watched and debated *To Kill a Mockingbird.* Organizational meetings to abolish racism. Regular visits by people as diverse as folksinger Pete Seeger and jazz balladeer Johnny Hartman, the only singer ever to record with the legendary John Coltrane. In fact, on one visit it was Hartman, noticing that the seven- or eight-year-old Chappelle had a knack for humor, who first planted the seed of his being a comedian.

"I was the funny dude. I was real comfortable with adults. I was cutting up in front of Hartman and he was like, 'Man, you're a funny kid.' And he says to me, 'You're gonna be a comedian.' And I was like, 'What's a comedian?' And he's like, 'It's a guy who tells funny stories for a living, like Richard Pryor or Redd Foxx.' I said, 'I want to be a doctor.' And he was like, 'Eh--' "

And why not? African-Americans of Chappelle's generation, carried along in the wake of the civil-rights movement, could be anything, they were told. For they were the first generation of blacks to be raised in an integrated America, to attend multiracial schools, to have friends of many backgrounds. "I use to hang out with the Jewish kids, Black kids, and Vietnamese immigrants," says Chappelle. The truth is, many African-American parents like Chappelle's struggled and sacrificed so that their children would not have to, so that they could attend a different kind of school, live in a different kind of neighborhood, dream a different kind of world. What they conceived, ultimately, was the first wave of African-Americans who were what the writer Trey Ellis once described as "cultural mulattoes." Born to two progressive black parents, one a we-are-the-world bohemian, the other firmly rooted in Black nationalism in Washington, D. C. ("Chocolate City," as dubbed by Parliament Funkadelic), Chappelle followed his father, during his middle-school years, to Yellow Springs, where his friends and his new family were suddenly, well, White, which created this unique capacity to stand out and blend in, to cross boundaries and set up roadblocks, to make fast friends and quick foes. Or, as the Black sage Dr. W. E. B. Du Bois wrote, "One ever feels his two-ness--an American, a Negro; two souls, two thoughts, two unreconciled strivings; two warring ideals in one dark body, whose dogged strength alone keeps it from being torn asunder."

On my last night in Yellow Springs, Chappelle takes a path foreign to me. When I ask him if this is the sixty-five-acre farm, his "anti-Hollywood estate," as one journalist coined it, Chappelle smiles mischievously and says, "Uh, this is one of my houses. I'm going to smash a rock over your head and take those tapes.

You'll never know which house I'm living in." Because it is pitch-black, save some strategically arranged lighting sprinkled about the property, all that can be said about Chappelle's real estate is that it is expansive.

Back on the familiar route, Chappelle noses the SUV through and around the empty streets of Yellow Springs with much on his mind. His face, creased with a smile just a second before, droops. He is a man with monumental decisions to make. The Comedy Central haze is so damn thick that Dave Chappelle wants to say, Fuck the world! all of it, but he knows that he cannot. It is evident now that there is pressure from all sides for him to return to the show, to pay off former associates (or deal with the legal consequences); that he is saddened by the wedge that has been driven between him and others, most notably Neal Brennan, his former longtime friend and writing partner on "Chappelle's Show." This is the crux of why Dave Chappelle left the show, why he went to Africa to breathe amid his stunning success, why he prefers life in Ohio. He doesn't like to feel, as an artist, as a comedian, as a black man in America, like he is being controlled, told what he should and should not be doing--ever. This is why, at the close of each episode of "Chappelle's Show," there is that image of a shirtless Chappelle with slave shackles on his wrists. This is why Chappelle prefers live stand-up to television, and especially to Hollywood films. And this is why, throughout the course of these final few hours together, Chappelle repeatedly brings up David Mamet's recent *Harper's* essay, "Bambi v. Godzilla: Why Art Loses in Hollywood," as well as Spike Lee's hotly debated flick "Bamboozled."

Then, out of the blue, he begins talking candidly, for the first time, about his conflicts with Comedy Central, his voice lower than before, his words coming a little more slowly.

"I don't want people to think that I feel completely victimized. Like, I always try to make a point of trying to acknowledge the fact that I made mistakes in this process. But believe me, I wasn't making 'em by myself. As a matter of fact, I had an enormous amount of help making mistakes. More help than I get when I'm doing the right thing.

"So basically the renegotiation during the show's second season was what it was. I felt like I was really pressured to settle for something that I didn't necessarily feel like I wanted. The DVD comes out, it's a whole 'nother ball game. Everyone's asking me, 'When you coming back, when you coming back? You'd do it for x number of dollars, wouldn't you?' Like, real specific questions, and it was like, I don't know. You know, I just got real tight-lipped about shit, because the same questions kept coming up over and over, you know, so when that happens, you stop assuming that these are idle questions. You start assuming that somebody wants to know something, and they're asking you via a bunch of different people. And if I would divulge that information, and I did want to come back, it would give me a very weak negotiating position if they knew what I would do something for. Common sense. 'Nigger be careful' is what they say on the streets, right?"

Chappelle asks me to turn off the tape recorder. Should he vent, should he be careful? He sparks a cigarette and continues. Between the first and second seasons, Comedy Central was sold. "There was a lot of new faces. Viacom had acquired the entire asset of Comedy Central. Certain things happened that were strange at the time." Chappelle straightens his back and mimics the voice of an older White executive: " 'Dave, we're having a symposium on the n-word, and we wanted you to speak about your use of it. It's just for our information.' And I did it, but afterward I was like, That was real stupid of me. Why the fuck would I explain to a room full of White people why I say the word nigga? Why on earth would I put myself in a position like that? So you got me on a panel, me and all of these, like, Harvard-educated, you know, upper-echelon authors, me, and a rapper. So here I am explaining, and I was real defensive 'cause of what was going on at the show at the time--we had just shot the Niggar Family sketch, and I was at a symposium on the word nigger. So I'm feeling like I'm fighting censorship. They say, 'We just want to know how far we should go with something like that.' And the subtext of it is, 'Do you want to know, or do you want to tell me something?'

"You have all these Harvard-educated people saying, 'I think the word is reprehensible' and talking about the destructive nature of blah, blah, blah. . . . You know, pontificating." Silence. A sigh.

"But the bottom line was, White people own everything, and where can a Black person go and be himself or say something that's familiar to him and not have to explain or apologize? Why don't I just take the show to BET--oh, wait a minute, you own that, too, don't you? Same thing happened with the Rick James episode. They gave us the notes and there were like forty-six or some insane number of bleeps that we would've had to put over it. 'Well, Dave, then why don't you go in and explain to them yourself.' So now I'm sitting in a room, again, with some White people, explaining why they say the n-word, and it's a sketch about Rick James, and I don't want to air a sketch with that many bleeps over it; it will render it completely ineffective. Give me another week and I'll just come up with something else. Run a rerun. 'No, we can't run a rerun, we've got ad buy-ins' and blah, blah, blah. Okay, well then, fine, I don't want to do it then. And so then there was a compromise. It was the only episode that aired with a disclaimer. But again, it was a position where I was explaining to white people why the n-word. It's an awful, awful position to put yourself in.

"I'm just saying it's a dilemma. It's something that is unique to us. White people, white artists, are allowed to be individuals. But we always have this greater struggle that we at least have to keep in mind somewhere."

Particularly if you, like Dave Chappelle, hail from a family of intellectuals and if you, like him, have been studying history since you were a child, are attuned to the world in a particular way, have a great-grandfather who is remembered in the Smithsonian Institution, and believe, in your heart, that you are a bridge builder between different cultures. That you can have close friends, like Neal Brennan, who are White, a wife who is Asian. That you have the right (and the bruises) to use the word nigga any way you choose. But at the same time, you feel that you also have a specific responsibility to Black America, that you have to think about the sights and sounds you put out there on television because you are not interested in being merely a source of enjoyment for White America at the expense of Black America. This is what occurs when black art goes pop, and that Black artist happens to have a functioning soul. One ever feels his two-ness--

For sure, it is Chappelle's birthright to talk, provocatively, in his art, about race in America. Yet somewhere in that process of journeying from a grossly underestimated comic to the funniest man in America, Dave Chappelle began to feel trapped by the reactions from the suits, from the fans, from the media from the scholars, from that voice inside his head. These jokes are dangerous in the wrong hands, he would say. That pressure, from all sides, from himself, would lead you, if you were living inside Dave Chappelle's head, to make a mad dash away from the money, real and projected, the fame, the pressures to do season three, of being labeled a brand, an icon, a genius. Just to think--

He drives on, through the dark Ohio night. "I'm in a much better place than I was when I went to Africa. And now things are starting to make more sense, like a fog that's lifting. But there's a part of me personally that's still like a work in progress. It's like the blood's rushing back into me. I feel more optimistic, more hopeful. But I still don't have the definitive course. People are thinking that I'm out here to avoid fame, and that's not it. What I'm trying to avoid is corruption."

And what of the relationship with Neal Brennan, who worked the door at Boston Comedy Club as Chappelle first began to make a name for himself? When Chappelle was in Africa,

Brennan told *Time* of an exchange he'd had with Chappelle, in which he said he had told the comic, "You're not well." Now parking on Xenia Avenue, the lone vehicle on the strip, Dave Chappelle pushes a sigh up from his chest, rolls his window up and down to blow out cigarette smoke, and weighs in on the question:

"I think Neal is a brilliant dude. We were close, man. These situations are intense. I'm sad. I'm not going to say I am angry. I was angry. The thing about show business is that, in a way, it forces dysfunctional relationships in people."

Chappelle falls dead silent one final time, not wanting to say too much about his former partner. Lights another cigarette. Blows. Talks again, becoming nostalgic as he fans the smoke and the subject away from Brennan.

"I have to say, it was by far the best experience I ever had working in television. When you hear me say, like, 'I quit' and all this stuff, I mean, that was literally just like the tension and the dramatic situation of creating something. And the network executives have their responsibilities and I have my responsibilities, so this is a natural tension of these relationships. By far, it was better than any situation I ever had in corporate television.

"It was like taking somebody on a tour through a young Black man's subconscious, and I don't think America has been there. So in a way it was kind of like reality TV, right"

As he steers his Toyota home, I ask him, if not "Chappelle's Show," then what is it that he wants to do next? Beaming with that mischievous grin again, Dave Chappelle tilts his head against the driver's seat, shoots smoke out of his mouth like an erupting volcano, then says, deadpan, "Spit hot fire."

He laughs. "I want to tell my jokes. I want to have time with my children. I want to entertain people. And at one point, I'll walk away from show business. But I don't want to walk away empty-handed."

Open Letter to Black America

APRIL 2010
PUBLISHED IN EBONY

Dear Black America:

This 42nd anniversary of the assassination of Dr. Martin Luther King, Jr. is an opportune moment to reflect on how far we've come, and how far we have to go. It calls us to reconsider the words Dr. King gave us at the end of his life, when he said that we need "a radical revolution of values." Certainly, we have much to be proud of. There is the first Black president. There are more Black elected officials, more Blacks in corporate America, the media, and in very real power positions, like Oprah Winfrey, Richard Parsons, Donna Brazile, and Jay-Z.

But, if we are to be brutally honest with ourselves, we've also got to acknowledge that things have not been right for some time. The civil rights era concept that our leaders would deliver us into the promised land has devolved into the idea that all we need to do is show up and follow. We have lost the sense of individual responsibility toward collective change.

Think back to the days immediately after slavery, when it was clear that Blacks wanted two things: education and land. In spite of vicious White terrorism, we plodded forward. There was hope, and a vocabulary of purpose. These values emboldened us during the Civil Rights Movement. And they were re-born during the 2008 presidential campaign. Yet, unlike before, many of us have failed to embrace the miraculous kind of self and community transformation that led us to walk, literally, into the teeth of barking dogs, water hoses, and police brutality, mainly because we refused to let anyone turn us around.

Why, politically, did we come out in record numbers for Barack Obama, then instantly return to apathy? Why do we remain suspended in a state of arrested development, believing that a dynamic leader will be our salvation? A civil rights veteran said it best to me many years ago: "We were just happy to get in the door. We never really had a plan beyond that." So we have to be honest and admit that Black leadership in America, except a few shining examples such as The Brotherhood/Sister Sol in New York City or John Hope Bryant's Operation Hope, has been too often stuck in yesterday. It has been unable to produce an agenda for Black America that will transform our communities in a holistic way. So we've spent 40 years like the Israelites, wandering the wilderness, harboring the misguided expectations that people like Barack, or Oprah, or anyone Black and famous will free us. It simply isn't going to happen.

And while we've been waiting, praying, and producing the same predictable conferences, summits, studies, and reports again and again, Black America is on the brink of catastrophe. We need to remind ourselves that Hurricane Katrina and Haiti's earthquake only magnify the slow forms of devastation happening each day. They include HIV and AIDS, poverty, Black self-hatred and Black-on-Black violence, the huge class divide, mediocre school systems, and the steady march of our youth into jails and cemeteries. We should stop saying this is a post-racial America because of President Obama. It is not. Despite Barack and Michelle we continue to be bombarded with destructive images of Black people in the mass media. As I travel the country speaking at universities and working for social justice, I note that our prisons are packed with black and brown bodies, and every American ghetto looks exactly the same: a lack of resources, services, and jobs, failing public schools, and limited access to the American dream.

That said, let us no longer wait on a savior to come. Do we want to continue wandering or do we want to create our future here and now? We have the power to transform our communities by enacting those "radical revolution of values." So I propose six things we must do immediately: Create a Spiritual Foundation; Move Toward Mental Wellness; Take Care of Our Physical Health; Become Politically Active; Understand the Power of Our Culture; and Start a Plan for Economic Empowerment.

Our spiritual foundation must be rooted in God or something greater than us, and a love for self and for all Black folks, unconditionally. It must grow out of our beliefs and our willingness to act selflessly. And it must begin with mental wellness because we cannot stand up for our convictions, our faith, or ourselves if our self-esteem is not in tact. Susan L. Taylor put it best when it comes to our mental health, Black America: healing is the new activism. Be it the increase in domestic violence, homicides and suicides, or the way so many of us say

"I can't" it is clear to me that since the civil rights period our individual and collective psyches have been damaged. But we can heal by seeking counseling and therapy, forming or joining positive support groups, and courageously ridding ourselves of toxic people, even if they are longtime friends, lovers, or kinfolk.

Physically, we can no longer accept that we are pre-destined for diabetes, high-blood pressure, and other ailments. Yes, like all Americans, we should have access to health care. But we should also change our diets and exercise regularly. Recently, my mother was hospitalized. After years of sitting on the sofa watching TV and indulging in terrible eating habits, that was her wake-up call. Change your diet and live. Don't change and die a painful and preventable death, as many of our relatives have.

Taking charge of our health and wellness also means changing the way we discuss our realities in America. Let us stop bemoaning our "crises" and start strategizing to meet our "challenges." Let us cease spreading reports that compare us unfavorably to our White sisters and brothers. Likewise, our culture, the way we talk, eat, sing, pray, dance, laugh, and cry must become more balanced so that it no longer reflects solely what is wrong with us, but also projects a vision of how great we can become, or are.

Financially, we've got to disconnect our self-esteem from our clothes and cars and instead focus on building true wealth. If my illiterate late grandparents could own land in South Carolina, by saving coins in their day, then we can, too. We can use our resources to empower ourselves, to help our 'hoods, and to support our people. This means doing more than donating to charity. It means a sincere and consistent giving back in terms of time, energy, and presence.

Black America, we've been surviving for 400 years in this nation. The question for the twenty-first century is this: Do we want to just survive, or do we want to win? The "radical" answers, if we search hard enough, are right there in our own hands.

Why I Support Gay Marriage

JUNE 2011
PUBLISHED IN DAILY KOS

My adopted home of New York is grappling with becoming the sixth (and most populous) American state to legalize gay marriage. Whether it happens or not, gay or same-sex marriage as a movement in America is here to stay. That is why I am saying very loudly, as a heterosexual male who plans on marrying the woman I love in the very near future, that I support gay marriage. And that I feel it should be the law in the entire United States one day. In short, I believe in human rights for all human beings. And equal protection under the law for all Americans. I have actually felt this way for a number of years, as I've spoken about equal rights and treatment for the lesbian, gay, bisexual, and transgender community in my speeches across America, and I've condemned homophobia and violence against the gay community in my writings. I have even made it a point to walk in gay pride parades, as a community and political leader, and I have participated in marches and rallies calling for safe spaces for the LGBT community in the aftermath of brutal attacks.

For me the reasons for these actions, through the years, are quite simple: I believe in equal rights for every human being; I believe that each and every one of us are sisters and brothers; and because of my own experiences, as a Black man, dealing with institutional and individual racism in America, to this day, I don't want to see any group oppressed, marginalized, discriminated against or ridiculed in the way my people have been. In other words, I am not just opposed to injustice that relates to me. I am opposed to any form of injustice that would stunt, hurt, or damage another human being, because I am so clear that we as a people are linked and if some of us are not free and empowered, then none of us are free and empowered. I think of this a great deal when I think of women and men I know, for fear of alienation, fear of losing a job or other opportunities, and for fear of being abused verbally or physically, or both, who simply keep their sexual orientation to themselves. That is just not the way to live, where you cannot be who you truly are. Just think of the emotional and spiritual toll that must take on a person's psyche. Could you imagine what your life would be like if you had to hide or repress parts of who you are, just to make others feel comfortable about themselves, or just to survive in a world hostile and opposed to your very existence? This is often very noticeable in our religious settings, be it churches, synagogues, or mosques. As an African American, I know the Black community is certainly not any more homophobic than any other part of America, and I reject any claims that we are. I've crisscrossed our country many times and have heard and witnessed horrific homophobia from people of various backgrounds. However, I do understand why many in my community are so outspoken on the issue of gay rights and gay marriage. We've been a people under siege since we were kidnapped from Africa and brought to these shores as slaves four centuries ago. We've seen our manhood and our womanhood denigrated and castrated from multiple angles. And we are a deeply proud people, proud of what we've survived, proud of what we've achieved, and proud of our relationship to whatever God we believe in (and yes, most of us do believe in God), against all odds. That does not leave much room for honest and open dialogue about sex, sexual orientation, or the abuse and misuse of sex in my community, as is the case in other communities, unless we struggle to build and create that room. And no room, no dialogue, typically means fear, misunderstanding, and, yes, even hatred of those who are "different."

But the grave danger of such a locked-in mindset is that right in our midst are individuals living their lives in guilt and shame because they feel, and they know, there are no safe spaces for healthy conversations on the many kinds of experiences that exist in the human family. Add in the constant barrage of negative and toxic sermonizing about gay people, including from pulpits every Sunday, and what we have is a deep inability and unwillingness to see the humanity in all of us, in spite of differences and disagreements.

I believe that is why so many in my community are hypersensitive to comparisons between the Civil Rights Movement and the gay rights movement. We as Black folks can never, for example, hide our skin color. But if one is White, or

White and gay, one can more readily move and excel in America because of the persistent reality of skin-color privilege, even if you are lesbian, gay, bisexual, or transgender. And I certainly know many lesbian, gay, bisexual, and transgender Black folks who complain of the racism within the gay community, even as the movement for gay marriage spreads, presumably for all gay people. It is my sincere hope that racism in the LGBT community is eventually dealt with openly and honestly, and in a way we straight folks have historically refused to do in America.

And it is my sincere hope that Black people, my people, begin to understand that the Civil Rights Movement, and most of our movements for justice and equality in America, dating back to slavery, have been so soulfully forceful and prophetic, that inevitably other people, other groups, would be inspired to fight for their own rights, too. But because so many of us are still deeply wounded by American racism, conversations about and comparisons to our struggles come across as diminishing or denigrating our very unique American journey.

But this goes both ways. I also challenge people in the gay marriage movement's leadership (the White leadership, that is) to really think about linking your very necessary movement to the Civil Rights Movement without ever having any real and consistent dialogue with responsible and open-minded Black leaders or other leaders of color. I clearly see a connection between each and every American movement for social justice, which is why I am an ally and supporter of the gay marriage movement. But many will not because there has not been any genuine and consistent outreach and dialogue on this issue.

Just the borrowing of language, tactics, and historical reference points is not enough.

The above notwithstanding, as a Christian I refuse to be a member of any church (or visit any religious institution, regardless of faith) that recklessly and aggressively condemns homosexuals, or any spiritual center which refers to homosexuality as a "sin," and seeks to "cure" gay people of their sexual orientation; and which, in one breath, talks about God and love yet in another breath preaches, directly or indirectly, hatred and ugliness toward gay people. Last time I checked none of us are God, none of us have had direct conversations with God, and the Christianity I believe in and practice is about love for all human beings. All means all.

Indeed, so many of us act as if gay sisters and brothers have not been in our lives and in this world until very recently. Well, they have been, and they have been a relative, a childhood friend, a hairdresser or a barber, a coworker or employer, a choir director (or even the pastor, rabbi, or imam), and they have been and are a part of every sector of American society and American history. Case in point, we often give Dr. King the major credit for the famous 1963 March on Washington, but it was actually a gay Black man named Bayard Rustin who spearheaded that historic event. But just as those who refuse to see them have habitually made Native Americans, Blacks, Latinos, Asians, women, the poor, and persons with disabilities invisible, the same has been and is the case with the gay community.

I was one of those individuals who refused to see or acknowledge the humanity of gay people until I began to actually hear to the voices of that community. In fact, that is precisely why I moved to New York City, because it truly is a rainbow, or what former Mayor David Dinkins called "a gorgeous mosaic" of human beings. Be it my cast mate Norman on the first season of MTV's "The Real World," or my first editor-in-chief and other staffers at Vibe magazine, or the many poets I've worked with in the literary scene, or the many painters, actors and actresses, singers and musicians I've crossed paths with, over time, as I listened and learned I heard tales of triumph and sorrow, of joy and pain, very similar to my own life journey. And all of us want the same things: a decent quality of life; decent and affordable housing; a job or career that makes us happy and that which brings us pride and dignity; and we all want love, love to give and love to receive, from family, and from an intimate partner, God and the universe willing.

My New York City journey led me, over time, to rethink my own homophobia (I was never a gay basher but I certainly had my fears and trepidations at one time), and it made me think about the former college mate of mine, a gay man, who allowed me to live with him and his teenage brother when I had no place to stay in the late 1980s. It made me think about Jonathan Van Meter, that first Vibe editor-in-chief who remains, to this day, the only person ever to give me a full-time job as a writer. It made me think of Michael Cummings, an openly gay visual artist in Harlem, who rented me a room in his brownstone when I lost everything after my Vibe years and was suffering through a terrible depression. And I think about the countless stories of gay sisters and brothers who have been verbally abused, physically assaulted, or killed for being who they are. For sure, the saddest funeral I've ever attended in my life was for Shani Baraka, daughter of famed poet Amiri Baraka, after she and her partner Rayshon were shot dead by the estranged husband of Shani's older sister. It was at that funeral, as I cried and cried, that I vowed I would become outspoken, as a straight person, about homophobia, and the awful hatred many gay people, be they out or not, have to confront daily.

For that reason I am not interested in tired, predictable debates about whether someone was born lesbian, gay, bisexual, or transgender, or if they "chose to be that way." I reject former New York Giant David Tyree's assertion that legalized gay marriage will lead to "anarchy." I know many same gender-loving couples, both male and female, which are raising children of their own, either by birth or adopted, and they are amazing parents. And, no, they are not "making their children be gay" as some are quick to suggest. Furthermore, this kind of ridiculous logic is what led many, back in the 1980s and early 1990s, to associate the AIDS virus solely with the gay community or, as I remember so clearly, many to think if they had an interaction of any kind with a gay person, no matter how innocent, "the gayness would rub off on them" or they would get the AIDS disease simply by touching or being in the same room or area as a gay person.

Fear is a not-so funny thing, particularly when it transforms itself into profound ignorance and hatred and some of us, again, start thinking we are God and, thus, can judge and condemn people. That is why I don't concern myself with Biblical quotes conveniently used to attack and condemn gay people, because I know that same Bible has been used to justify, say, American slavery, or the subordination of women. What I do know is that just how it was once illegal for Blacks and Whites to marry in many states in this country, and it is morally wrong for us, in the 21st century, in our democracy, to tell people who they can and cannot love, or marry, because we want, fear and hateful reactions firmly in our hearts, to determine what love and marriage is for every single individual.

For those with selective amnesia love is an unfiltered expression of devotion to another human being. Marriage is simply the legal and official confirmation of that devotion. I know many gay couples who've been together for years, for decades, even, but because they cannot legally wed in most American states, they do not have the legal and economic protections of women and men married to each other. Yet they have relationships stronger and far more committed than many heterosexual couples I know personally.

And because none of us, not you, not me, can tell anyone who and how they should love, I say now is the time to come into the 21st century and acknowledge, at this historic moment, that we are all children of whatever God or Goddess we believe in (or not, and we have that right, too), all creatures of this universe, and that if our nation, and our planet, is to truly move forward, then it is time to create safe spaces for love and marriage for all people, equally.

A Poem for Anita Hill

written on the occasion of the 20th anniversary of Ms. Hill's testimony at the Supreme Court hearings of Clarence Thomas in October 1991

OCTOBER 2011
PUBLISHED IN MS. MAGAZINE

miss anita hill
what happens
when a woman
dares to split
her lips and use
the tongue
the universe
and the ancestors
gave her to
fingerpop the flesh
from lies
and expose
the truth
of a manhood

gone mad

?

miss anita hill

i thank you

as a man

for being

one of my teachers

for having the bottomless bravery

of sojourner truth

susan b. anthony

helen keller

ida b. wells

annie besant

frida kahlo

dorothy height

eleanor roosevelt

simone de beauvoir

fannie lou hamer

ella baker

audre lorde

angela davis

bella abzug

sonia sanchez

gloria steinem

susan taylor

alice walker

bell hooks

eve ensler

patti giggans

shelley serdahely

ani difranco

lynn nottage

debby tucker

april silver

dj kuttin kandi

dj beverly bond

cheyla mccornack

malia lazu

aishah shahidah simmons

laura dawn

pratibha parmar

maisha morales

richelle carey

blanca elizabeth vega

asha bandele

jessica care moore

my grandmother

my mother

my aunties

and all the women

whose names

we will never know

and all the women

who are not yet born

miss anita hill
do you know the
saga of my mother
a young woman
birthed from the scorn
of the old American South
oppressive Carolina clay of Jim
Crow
hammered between her toes
with poverty and gloom
bookending the braided hair
of her youth—
first chance she got my ma
borrowed a greyhound
bus ride to freedom
worked odd jobs
like the one where
a rich man, a rich white man,
thought it his civic duty
to erase his skin of
everything except
his robe and his penis
sat on the synthetic sofa with
his legs wide open
so my mother could
see his private parts
they didn't call it

sexual harassment
back then in the early 1960s
they called it a job
and if you wanted
to keep that job
you had to scotch-tape
the disgust gushing from
your throat and pretend
your womanhood had
not just been used
and discarded like a
soda can with pubic
hair spit-stuck to the rim

miss anita hill
what about my friend
who, just two weeks ago,
did the good deed of
checking on one of
the young people
from her youth program
because the girl's school
asked her to
little did my friend know
that she was moonwalking
into the den of
a dream deferred named stepfather

a poor man, a poor black man
he didn't like the questions
my friend was asking
him about the girl
so his manhood threw
kitchen chairs at my friend
like they were nuclear missiles
and when he had abused
those chairs he took the pieces
of the chairs and beat
my friend with those
when the pieces had
disintegrated in his hellish hands
he beat my friend with his fists
slapboxing with jesus
one rapper called it
except stepfather
wasn't jesus he was the devil—
a devil in redwhiteblue boxing
trunks
and my friend an unwilling sparring
partner
stepfather jabbed and sucker-
punched
my friend with body blows
beat her across the face
as her braces stabbed and
daggered the gums

of her mouth, the blood
bumrushing her brain the
way them busted levees
flooded new orleans in '05
miss anita hill, could
you hear her sorrow songs
for him to stop?
could you see the songs
of freedom in her black-and-blue
eyes
as she slapboxed
with the devil, every hit
he gave she returned best she could
determined that her funeral
would not be in the rotted and
ruined
home of a madman?
but stepfather beat my friend so bad
that the 16-year-old girl
stood upright and frozen
in the track-marks of
her own nightmare
for 3 long years
stepfather had raped
this girl like it was
his divine order to do so
for 3 long years
stepfather had beaten

this girl like it was
his destiny to be a
domestic terrorist
9-1-1 the girl
called 9-1-1
to rescue not only my
friend but herself
she called 9-1-1
as stepfather slashed
and burned
my friend's clothes from her body
and readied his penis for invasion
the girl called 9-1-1
as my friend's mind and
bones were body-slammed by
trauma
and the greasy, sweat-stained floor
prepared itself for the receipt of her
life
and it was right then that
the police came through the door—

miss anita hill
my friend spent a week
at a rape recovery center
she and that 16-year-old girl
I learned all of this
when my friend texted me

one day sharing what happened
she had been hung so high
from a shock tree
that she could not remember if
it happened on a
thursday or friday
but it was one of those
days, she was sure
miss anita hill
the stepfather is in
jail now and that girl
has been freed from her
prison
just the way
you've liberated so many
women and girls
from man-made boxes
20 long years ago
simply by having
the audacity to
set sexism on fire
miss anita hill
have you ever thought
of how many women
and girls would not
be free now if
your voice had
not freed them?

you are like
harriet tubman
your life
the underground railroad
that has taken
so many to a place
they did not know exist

and when the
closing chapters of your
life are penciled into the moon
miss anita hill
they will say
that you were a human
being a woman
a black woman
a sister a friend
a leader a mentor
a teacher who
they tried to mock and malign
and crush and defeat
who they
said did not see
what she saw
did not feel what she
felt but who
because of the
convictions in her

lone tree, oklahoma soul
got up anyway
because that is
what the selfless do
they martyr
even their own
sanity their own lives
and in so doing
they know they
birth a child called change
a new birth day
a new v-day
where women and girls
like you, miss anita hill
like my mother
like my grandmother
and my aunts
like my friend
and that 16-year-old girl
and all the women
and girls whose names
we will never know
can say I too can be
free I too can use
my power and my voice
because miss anita hill
said so—

BARACK OBAMA, RONALD REAGAN, AND THE GHOST OF DR. KING

Made in Our America: Letter to Trayvon Martin

APRIL 2012
PUBLISHED IN ALTERNET.ORG

Dear Trayvon:

What do I say to you, man-child, or for you, that has not already been said? I've tried writing this letter to you several times, and several times the words would not come. There have been tears in their place, or immense anger, and a painfully heavy kind of sorrow. Or some debilitating element of fear, if I can be vulnerable and real with you. Fear that I might say the wrong thing, or somehow offend you, your family, or someone who may not agree with my views of our society. But this is not a time to be afraid, Trayvon. We are past that now, and we know that being afraid to speak and do is the same as creating your own prison, and being stuck there forever. These times are demanding courage, vision, love, and the determination to make sure your death is not in vain. For in writing this letter to you I am also writing it to myself, to America, to all of us, and asking myself, all of us, our America, to be truthful, in a way we have not been previously, about who we are. Your murder,

Trayvon, is a national tragedy, and the entire world's gaze is upon us with a mixture of empathy and disappointment. Empathy because any human being, regardless of her or his background, and unless they lack a sense of humanity, is going to feel the devastating loss of a life, even that of a stranger. Disappointment because we in America claim to be a democracy, one that sets the standard for other countries—a great nation where there is, allegedly, justice and equality for each and everyone—yet it took over six weeks for George Zimmerman to be arrested, and only because of loud and very consistent public outcries. And Mr. Zimmerman may have been the man who pulled the trigger, but there are so many responsible for your life ending, abruptly, at the age of 17, Trayvon. You did not deserve to die that young, not like that, in the frightened and tormented darkness of that Sunday evening in late February.

Furthermore Trayvon, I need to state, without hesitation, to those who have been quick to say that folks like me are screaming racism for the heck of it, that I love people, no matter who they are, that I really do believe there is just one race, the human race, that we are, each of us, sisters and brothers in the human family. And I do not simply condemn racism. I also denounce sexism, classism, religious intolerance and disrespect, homophobia, a reckless disregard and bigotry toward persons with disabilities, and violence in any way—in short every form of hatred and human-to-human madness one can name. We cannot merely be opposed to wrong and injustice that is convenient for us. We must also be opposed to every single kind of wrong and injustice, even if it does not directly touch or affect our lives.

Because, eventually, it will. And because we human beings are ultimately connected, whether we want to accept that truth or not.

Trayvon, due to my own challenges and changes, it took me many years to come to this conclusion, but after many conversations with my God, countless spiritual and emotional journeys, and travels to and interactions with communities and individuals worlds apart from the experiences of Black boys like you and I, I do believe there are things that bind us, regardless of skin color, or culture, or ethnicity, or region or national boundaries. Like our faith in something greater than ourselves that creates and sustains us. Like our desire to be happy, to have a stable home, a family. Like our longing to have possibilities for ourselves, our loved ones, and for employment that is not merely to pay the bills or survive financially, but actually brings us pride and dignity. I would like to believe, Trayvon, that somewhere in the isolation and confusion of George Zimmerman's heart and mind, this man, born of a White father and a Latina mother, is not that different from you or I. Indeed, if America is to ever heal and grow from the centuries of violence, murder, mayhem, and ugly and utterly unnecessary divides passed from generation to generation so effortlessly, like plates of food at the family barbeque, then, yes, we must learn to love, Trayvon, and forgive, including those whose ignorance and hatred is so deeply etched upon their souls that they would first think to aim a gun, fist, or insult at us rather than a kind or loving gesture.

So there is never sunshine, or a rainbow, until after the storm has passed. The storm America has been avoiding for so long is a very real and necessary conversation on race and racism. For racism is the greatest cancer in our nation's skin, and it is as rooted in the American psyche as the Declaration of Independence, the Constitution, the Emancipation Proclamation, and the Civil Rights Movement. Anyone who suggests otherwise, Trayvon, does not know the America we know. They claim to be patriots, claim to represent the best of what America is or can be, yet they simultaneously harass people like me in email and on Facebook and Twitter with the same kind of racist language that was thrown at our ancestors as they were marching and demanding the very basic freedoms of citizenship and the right to vote in the 1950s and 1960s. In America racism is about power, it is about privilege, and it is about image and perception. That means at the end of the day it ultimately don't mean a thing if George Zimmerman is White, or Latino, or a combination of both, or if he were Black, either: God knows I have witnessed my share of Black police officers since I was your age Trayvon, for example, who methodically brutalized young Black males in America's ghettoes, especially, for no good reason, in broad daylight, as the boys lay helpless on the ground with hands cuffed behind their backs. Some Black cops, like George Zimmerman, have internalized the racism, have come to believe what the dominant White culture (yes, those certain White males with power and privilege who control images and perceptions, most of our images and perceptions) say about Black males, dating back to the human raiding of Africa and slavery: That we are menaces to the American republic and, accordingly, must be contained and controlled, with the power of position, or with the power of guns and laws that always seem to adversely endanger Black men and boys like you and I, Trayvon. So it was your race, your dark complexion that mattered that night, not your hooded sweatshirt. It does not matter that there are some, reading this right this moment, that will dispute or denigrate my words, say I am harking back to a bygone era. I am talking to you, Trayvon, not them, and I am speaking with people who know how to listen and laugh and love as you did, Trayvon. I am talking to those who would never insist that any people should simply erase the memory and pain of their history because they do not want to hear it any longer. Simply because their lack of humanity has led them to pretend things have changed so much that they can move on with business as usual, or as if none of it matters in 21st century America. Well, it does, Travyon. If it did not, then why are you dead, my friend? Trayvon, we will simply pray for folks like that and wish them well. Moreover, what does matter is the mentality of racism that was festering within Mr. Zimmerman, a mentality that taught him to view Black males, specifically, as suspicious, as criminals. Where Mr. Zimmerman received that education—his White father with his military and law resume, his mostly White neighborhood in Virginia, the school system, the mass media and pop culture machinery, his co-workers or employers through the years, that gated and mostly White community in Sanford, Florida— doesn't actually matter. What matters is he got it just the way most Americans get our lessons about people who are different from us: in a way that elevates difference over similarity, that pushes fear and hate instead of respect and love, that opts for violence when nonviolence should always be the first and only weapon we ever use.

You knew none of this, Trayvon, as you were walking with a bag of Skittles and a can of iced tea in your hands. But you were a walking dead man-child the moment George Zimmerman ignored the police dispatcher's order not to pursue you. In that moment, Mr. Zimmerman had become your judge, your juror, and your executioner in a single bound of racist logic. Your life, gone. The final waves of magic of Barack Obama's historic 2008 election, gone. Myths and lies that America had become a post-racial society, gone. Pretensions and denials that Black people can live in gated suburban communities and not think about being Black each minute of their existence, gone. But this is not new, Trayvon, what happened to you. It really began when Martin Luther King, Jr. and the Civil Rights Movement were still alive. Not only are you the modern-day Emmett Till, but you are also the four little girls bombed to death in Alabama; the scores of Black and White civil rights workers murdered for having the audacity to come together, for freedom, for democracy, for America. And you are a victim of the policies of President Ronald Reagan and the Reagan era, too, Trayvon. I remember those times well. Mr. Reagan may have been the so-called great communicator and symbolic leader of America's late 20th century conservative movement, but it was in the 1980s that the seeds were sown for "taking back our country," which manifest themselves today in the Tea

Party, in anti-democracy voter identification laws snaking their way from state to state—one well-financed piece of legislation after another, in the nonstop attacks on the rights and bodies of women, and in the anti-immigration fanaticism masked as protecting our borders and our traditions. Anyone who cannot see the connections between these multiple efforts, the energies channeled to divide and conquer, to pit Americans against each other, against ourselves and our own interests, Trayvon, can easily become George Zimmerman and patrol a neighborhood because they have been so contaminated with hate and rage that they do not realize they are no longer thinking for themselves—

And what you wanted was a bag of Skittles and a can of iced tea and you got death instead...

This land is our land, Trayvon, from one Native American reservation to the next, from ghetto to ghetto, from ocean to ocean, from one long unemployment line or long gas line to the next. We have a Black president in the White House and a Black boy, you, whose execution was so preposterous that even he, Barack Obama, finally had to admit that you could have been his son. Yet the president's slow response time, Trayvon, is a symptom of American racism. Black elected officials, more times than not, and particularly in these times, if they want to get re-elected, are generally not free to speak their minds on sensitive subjects like race, nor free to be the whole, well-rounded, and complex beings that God made them to be. Nor free to be, well, their Black selves... So many, except the ones with guts of steel and more concern for truth than poll numbers and political careers, silence themselves or speak with forked tongues, stick their hands in their pockets, and strike race-neutral poses as often as possible. That, to me, is as demented as the behavior of George Zimmerman, or the Tea Party, or the remarkably offensive Republican primary comments of Newt Gingrich, Mitt Romney, and Rick Santorum. Equally demented, Trayvon, are some of the so-called progressives or liberals who do not get the position a Barack Obama is in, how he really will never be, as president, the kind of candidate he was, because the office of the presidency is already very restrictive. Add the dynamic of Mr. Obama's race, or biracialism, and you have a man who appears, Trayvon, to some, to have lost his swagger, to be, well, powerless to champion and deliver that hope and that change so eloquently guaranteed in what feels like an eternity ago.

Perhaps that is why America turns, again and again, to the ghost of Dr. King. Our collective soul is so repressed at times that a dead man has more vision and more answers than we do. That just should not be the case any longer, because Dr. King is never coming back, Trayvon. And neither are you, young man. But what is here, what Martin Luther King left, and what you've left, Trayvon Martin, is a call to action for our souls, and for the soul of America. What connects you to Dr. King is that he, and Ella Baker, and Fannie Lou Hamer, and Malcolm X and nameless or forgotten others, fought, sacrificed, died, Trayvon, so that my generation and your generation could move freely, anywhere in America. Yet 44 years since MLK was shot on that Memphis motel balcony the way you were shot in that Florida gated community, we know that is not the case. Further irony, Trayvon, is that if you were in a ghetto environment your fear would not have been a George Zimmerman but someone of your own race. Yes, internalized racism and Black self-hatred are real, and we should be as angry about that as we are about what George Zimmerman did to you. There is no room in the process called soul searching for selective outrage. But any society that is forever chasing its tail instead of mustering the courage to stand still and look itself in the mirror will do exactly that. For sure, I asked once in a poem "where does one run to when stuck in the promised land?" Well, the answer, Trayvon, is that we should not be running at all. That we should be living, and loving each other and ourselves as if the future of the world depends on our commitment to such. Because it does, young man, it really does.

Finally, Trayvon, I need to leave you with something an older man said to me when I was but a few years older than you. That you are a prince. A prince because your tragic death has given many the chance to see light for the first time, to feel and be in a very different way. While some may criticize those who wear hoodies in your honor, I say at least they are doing something. My beef is with the ones who do nothing but talk, if they do that. We've got enough talkers and non-doers in our America, plenty of individuals who think of themselves and not others, ever. But your death will not be in vain, Trayvon, if we are able to gently nudge those types aside and make way for the folks who know we will not only get full justice for you, but who will take America forward, not back. You, wherever you are today, do not be afraid ever again, of George Zimmerman, of the dark, of walking wherever you please, Trayvon. They can kill a man-child, a boy, in cold blood, they can leave him for dead, they can delay informing his parents, they can hope the sorry episode would disappear, but they cannot murder his spirit. And they will never be completely free if all of us are not completely free—

Kevin

Acknowledgements

I would like to thank Lauren Summers, Rob Kenner, Danielle Lewis, Donald Garner, Penny Wrenn, Sherehe Hollins, and Lasana Hotep who all, at various times, offered great editorial advice and critical eyes to some of the blogs and essays in this collection. I would also like to thank the following media outlets for originally publishing the pieces in this book between the years 2006 and 2012: Esquire Magazine, Daily Kos, Huffington Post, The Women's Media Center, Ebony Magazine, allhiphop.com, bet.com, Uptown Magazine, Clutch Magazine, OpEdNews, theroot.com, The Daily Voice, daveyd.com, BlackPlanet.com, The Guardian, Ms. Magazine, and so many other websites and blog spaces I simply cannot recall right this moment. But please know I appreciate each one of you.

I most certainly need to thank the great team who've made this book possible: the visionaries at Lulu.com, including Bob Young, Tom Bright, Shanon Lewis, Daniel Wideman, AJ McDonald, and Allison Casey; Marisa King-Redwood of Buzz Brand Marketing (my management) and April Silver of AKILA WORKSONGS (my publicity and marketing); and the creative geniuses Kerry DeBruce (graphic designer) and Carl Posey (photographer). Finally, I would like to acknowledge, salute, and thank the people, in America and globally, who took it upon themselves to post or re-post, to tweet or re-tweet, many of these blogs and essays on Facebook, Twitter, Linkedin, and other social networking sites. You have no idea how much your support means to me—

CPSIA information can be obtained at www.ICGtesting.com
Printed in the USA
LVOW11s0058080116

469669LV00004B/518/P